WHAT IS THE BOOK OF ROMANS?

Kids' Guides to God's Word Series

What Is the Book of Genesis?
What Is the Book of Exodus?
What Is the Book of Leviticus?
What Is the Book of Numbers?
What Is the Book of Deuteronomy?
What Is the Book of Joshua?
What Is the Book of Judges?
What Is the Book of Ruth?
What Is the Book of 1 Samuel?
What Is the Book of 2 Samuel?
What Is the Book of 1 Kings?
What Is the Book of 2 Kings?
What Are the Books of 1–2 Chronicles?
What Are the Books of Ezra & Nehemiah?
What Is the Book of Esther?
What Is the Book of Job?
What Is the Book of Psalms?
What Is the Book of Proverbs?
What Is the Book of Ecclesiastes?
What Are the Books of Song of Songs & Lamentations?
What Is the Book of Isaiah?
What Is the Book of Jeremiah?
What Is the Book of Ezekiel?
What Is the Book of Daniel?
What Are the Books of Hosea–Micah?
What Are the Books of Nahum–Malachi?
What Is the Gospel of Matthew?
What Is the Gospel of Mark?
What Is the Gospel of Luke?
What Is the Gospel of John?
What Is the Book of Acts?
What Is the Book of Romans?
What Is the Book of 1 Corinthians?
What Is the Book of 2 Corinthians?
What Is the Book of Galatians?
What Is the Book of Ephesians?
What Is the Book of Philippians?
What Are the Books of Colossians & Philemon?
What Are the Books of 1–2 Thessalonians?
What Are the Books of 1–2 Timothy & Titus?
What Is the Book of Hebrews?
What Is the Book of James?
What Are the Books of 1–2 Peter & Jude?
What Are the Books of 1-3 John?
What Is the Book of Revelation?

What Is the Book of

ROMANS?

Michael Whitworth

ISBN 978-1-941972-51-9

Published by Start2Finish
Bend, Oregon 97702
start2finish.org

Printed in the United States of America

30 29 28 27 26 1 2 3 4 5

CONTENTS

INTRODUCTION

Have you ever received a letter that changed how you saw everything? Maybe it was a note from someone who believed in you when you didn't believe in yourself. Maybe it was a message that explained something you'd been confused about for years, and suddenly the whole picture snapped into focus. Maybe it was just a few sentences from the right person at the right time, and after reading them, you were different.

The book of Romans is that kind of letter. It was written nearly two thousand years ago by a man named Paul to a church he had never visited, in a city he had never seen. And it turned the world upside down.

Romans has been called the most important letter ever written. That's not an exaggeration. When a North African theologian named Augustine read Romans in the fourth century, it broke him open and made him one of the most influential thinkers in Christian history. When a German monk named Martin Luther wrestled with Romans in the sixteenth century, it sparked a revolution that reshaped the church and changed the course of Western civilization. When a preacher named

John Wesley heard someone reading from Luther's preface to the letter to the Romans in 1738, his heart was "strangely warmed," and a movement was born that swept across England and America.

This letter has that kind of power. Not because Paul was a gifted writer (though he was), but because the message he carried is the most explosive truth the world has ever heard: that the God who made you, the God you have failed, the God whose justice you cannot satisfy, has done something about it himself. He has provided a way for guilty people to be declared righteous, for enemies to become children, for the hopeless to be given a future that nothing in the universe can take away.

That message is called the gospel. And Romans is its fullest explanation.

WHO WROTE THIS, AND WHY?

Paul was not always a Christian. Before he met Jesus, he was a Pharisee, one of the strictest religious leaders in Israel. He studied the Scriptures. He kept the law with fierce precision. And when followers of Jesus began claiming that a crucified man had risen from the dead, Paul made it his mission to destroy them. He arrested believers. He approved of their executions. He was, by his own admission, the church's most violent enemy.

Then Jesus appeared to him on a road to Damascus, and everything changed. The man who had tried to stamp out the faith became its most tireless messenger. For the next twenty-five years, Paul traveled thousands of miles across the Roman Empire, planting churches, writing letters, and preaching the gospel to anyone who would listen.

By the time he wrote Romans, around AD 57, Paul was planning a trip to Spain to preach the gospel in places it had never been heard. He hoped to stop in Rome along the way and meet the Christians there. But he had never visited them before, and he knew that some had questions about his message. Was grace really free? Did it matter whether you were Jewish or Gentile? If salvation was by faith, did the law still matter? And what about Israel, God's chosen people, who had mostly rejected their own Messiah?

So Paul sat down and wrote them the gospel. Not a quick summary. Not a casual greeting. A careful, thorough, breathtaking explanation of what God has done to rescue the human race. It's the closest thing we have to Paul sitting across the table from you and saying, "Let me tell you everything."

WHAT YOU'RE ABOUT TO READ

Here's a roadmap of where we're headed:

The Gospel in One Sentence (Romans 1:1–17). Paul introduces himself and the message that drives his entire life: the gospel is the power of God for salvation to everyone who believes.

The Verdict No One Wants to Hear (Romans 1:18–3:20). Before the good news can mean anything, you have to understand the bad news. Paul proves that every person on earth—whether openly sinful, quietly self-righteous, or deeply religious—stands guilty before God. No one is innocent. No one has an excuse.

The Gift No One Earned (Romans 3:21–4:25). Then comes the turn. God has provided a righteousness that doesn't come from human effort but from his own grace, received through faith. Paul uses Abraham as living proof that this has always been God's way.

Peace with God (Romans 5). Justified people receive peace with God, access to grace, hope in suffering, and the assurance that God's love was proven at the cross. Paul also compares Adam and Christ, showing that what one man's sin destroyed, another man's obedience restored, and then some.

Dead to Sin (Romans 6). If grace is free, should we keep sinning so grace can keep growing? Paul's answer is explosive: absolutely not. Christians have died with Christ and been raised to a new life. The old self is gone.

The War Inside (Romans 7). But the Christian life isn't simple. Paul describes the agonizing struggle of someone who knows what is right, wants to do what is right, and still can't pull it off. The law reveals the problem but can't solve it.

Nothing Can Separate Us (Romans 8). This is the chapter everything has been building toward. Life in the Spirit. No condemnation. Adoption as God's children. A creation groaning for redemption. And the unshakable promise that absolutely nothing in all creation can separate us from the love of God in Christ Jesus.

Has God Given Up on Israel? (Romans 9–11). Paul wrestles with the hardest question his gospel raises: if most of Israel rejected Jesus, has God's word failed? His answer defends God's faithfulness, distinguishes between election to service and election to salvation, and ends in a hymn of praise to the depth of God's wisdom.

What the Gospel Looks Like on Monday Morning (Romans 12–13). Theology becomes Tuesday. Paul shows what a grace-shaped life looks like: living sacrifices, renewed minds, genuine love, overcoming evil with good, respecting authorities, and waking up to the urgency of the time.

Living Together in Grace (Romans 14–16). Finally, Paul addresses what happens when Christians disagree about secondary issues. His answer is not "win the argument" but "welcome one another, just as Christ welcomed you." The letter closes with personal greetings, a warning about division, and a doxology that brings everything full circle.

WHY THIS MATTERS FOR YOU

You might wonder why a letter written to first-century Romans matters to your life today. Here's why: the questions Romans answers are the same questions every generation asks.

Am I guilty? Yes. Every person who has ever lived has fallen short of what God designed us to be. Romans doesn't let anyone off the hook.

Can I be forgiven? Yes. Not by earning it, not by being good enough, not by belonging to the right group, but by trusting the God who did for you what you could never do for yourself. That's grace. And it changes everything.

Does God really love me? Yes. And the proof isn't a feeling. It's a fact. Christ died for you while you were still his enemy. That kind of love doesn't depend on your performance. It depends on his character.

What do I do now? You live. You offer your body as a living sacrifice. You let the Spirit transform your mind. You love the people around you, even the ones who are hard to love. You stop trying to impress God and start resting in what he has already done.

BEFORE YOU BEGIN

Romans is not an easy book. Parts of it are dense. Some sections require you to slow down and read carefully. Paul builds arguments the way an architect builds a cathedral: every piece supports every other piece, and if you skip a section, you might miss how the whole thing holds together.

But here's what I want you to know: this book was not written for scholars. It was written for ordinary Christians in an ordinary city, people who were trying to figure out what the gospel meant for their real, everyday lives. Paul wrote for them. And he wrote for you.

So take your time. Read the chapters in order. Don't skip ahead. Let Paul build his case the way he intended, one brick at a time. By the end, you won't just know more about God. You'll know more about yourself, about the world, and about the love that holds both together.

The most important letter ever written is in your hands.

Turn the page.

1

THE GOSPEL IN ONE SENTENCE

Have you ever tried to explain something huge in just a few words? Maybe a friend asks what your favorite movie is about, and you realize the whole story is so layered that a quick summary can't do it justice. You try anyway. You boil it down to one sentence, and somehow that one sentence captures the heart of the whole thing.

That's what Paul does in the opening verses of Romans. Before he unpacks one of the longest, deepest, most carefully argued letters in the entire Bible, he gives us the whole message in miniature. It's like a movie trailer for the rest of the book. Everything Paul will spend sixteen chapters explaining is already here, packed into seventeen verses like a seed that contains an entire tree.

But before we get to the message, we need to meet the messenger.

THE MAN BEHIND THE LETTER

Paul didn't start out as a Christian. He started out as the

opposite. Before he met Jesus, Paul was a Pharisee, one of the most devout religious groups in Israel. He studied the Scriptures. He kept the law with fierce precision. And when a group of Jews started claiming that a crucified man named Jesus had risen from the dead and was the Messiah, Paul was furious. He considered them dangerous heretics, and he made it his personal mission to shut them down.

He went house to house in Jerusalem, dragging believers off to prison. He watched approvingly when a man named Stephen was stoned to death for preaching about Jesus. Then he got official letters authorizing him to travel to Damascus and arrest more Christians there.

He never made it to Damascus as a persecutor. On the road, a blinding light knocked him to the ground and a voice spoke: "Saul, Saul, why do you persecute me?" It was Jesus. The very person Paul was trying to destroy turned out to be alive, and Paul's entire world collapsed and rebuilt itself in a single moment.

From that day forward, Paul was a different man. The man who had tried to destroy the church became its most tireless champion. He traveled thousands of miles across the Roman Empire, planting churches, writing letters, and preaching the message he had once tried to silence.

By the time he wrote Romans, Paul had been at this for about twenty-five years. He had preached across modern-day Turkey, Greece, and beyond. He had been beaten, shipwrecked, imprisoned, and chased out of more cities than he could count. And now he was writing to a church in the most important city in the world: Rome.

There was just one problem. He had never been there.

WRITING TO STRANGERS

Paul didn't start the church in Rome. We don't know exactly who did. It's possible that Jewish believers who were present at Pentecost carried the message back to the capital. However it happened, by the time Paul wrote this letter, there was a thriving Christian community in Rome made up of both Jewish and Gentile believers.

Paul had wanted to visit them for years. He mentions it in the letter itself: he had made plans to come many times but kept getting prevented. His work in the eastern part of the empire always seemed to need just a little more time. Now he was planning a trip to Spain and hoped to stop in Rome along the way. But in case he couldn't make it in person, he decided to do the next best thing.

He would write them the gospel.

Not a short note. Not a quick greeting. A full, careful, thorough explanation of the most important message in the history of the world. That's what Romans is. It's Paul's masterpiece, the most complete presentation of the Christian gospel anywhere in the New Testament.

And it begins the way all ancient letters began: with the sender introducing himself.

SLAVE, APOSTLE, SET APART

"Paul, a servant of Christ Jesus, called to be an apostle, set apart for the gospel of God." That's the very first verse, and it tells you three things about Paul that explain everything he's about to say.

First, he calls himself a servant. The word he used actually means "slave." In the Roman world, a slave was someone who belonged completely to another person. They had no rights of their own. Their entire life was defined by their master's will. Paul is saying, "I belong to Jesus. My life is not my own. Everything I do, I do because he owns me."

That might sound harsh, but Paul didn't see it that way. He was a slave who served willingly, out of love. He had been rescued by Jesus, and he responded by giving Jesus everything. His time, his energy, his plans, his future. All of it belonged to Christ.

Second, Paul says he was "called to be an apostle." An apostle was someone personally chosen and sent by Jesus to speak with his authority. Paul wasn't self-appointed. He didn't apply for the job. Jesus appeared to him on that road to Damascus and drafted him into service. This matters because everything Paul writes in Romans carries the weight of that calling. He's not sharing personal opinions. He's delivering a message entrusted to him by Christ himself.

Third, Paul says he was "set apart for the gospel of God." This is the phrase that sets the entire letter in motion. Paul's whole life had one focus: the gospel. That word means "good news," and Paul believed it was the most important announcement ever made.

Notice whose gospel it is. It's "the gospel of God." Paul didn't make it up. He didn't borrow it from another religion. It came from God himself.

A PROMISE KEPT

Paul immediately connects the gospel to something much older than himself: "the gospel he promised beforehand through his prophets in the Holy Scriptures."

This is a crucial point, and Paul makes it right at the start. The gospel wasn't a surprise. It wasn't some brand-new idea that appeared out of nowhere when Jesus showed up. God had been promising it for centuries through the Old Testament prophets. The entire story of Israel, from Abraham to Moses to David to the exile, was building toward this moment.

Think of it this way. If the gospel were a movie, the Old Testament would be the longest trailer in history, stretching across thousands of years. Promise after promise, prophecy after prophecy, all pointing forward to something God was going to do. And now, Paul says, the wait is over. The movie has arrived.

What is the gospel about? Paul answers immediately: "regarding his Son."

The gospel is about Jesus. It's not a philosophy. It's not a self-help program. It's not a list of rules for being a good person. It's an announcement about a person: God's Son.

Paul then describes Jesus in two ways that would have electrified his first readers. First, Jesus "was a descendant of David." That's a claim about his humanity and his identity as the Messiah. For centuries, the Jews had expected a king from David's line who would rule forever. God had promised David that one of his descendants would sit on an eternal throne. Paul is saying: Jesus is that king.

Second, Jesus was "appointed the Son of God in power by his resurrection from the dead." Before the resurrection, Jesus walked the earth in weakness, in humility, in the vulnerability of an ordinary human life. He was rejected. He suffered. He died on a cross. But when God raised him from the dead, everything changed. The resurrection was like a divine announcement to the universe: this man is who he claimed to be. He is the Son of God, and he now reigns with power that will never end.

Those two descriptions capture the whole story. David's descendant, born in humility. God's Son, raised in glory. Weakness and power. The cross and the empty tomb. That's the gospel in miniature.

A DEBT TO PAY

After describing the gospel, Paul explains his mission. Through Jesus, he says, "we received grace and apostleship to call all the Gentiles to the obedience that comes from faith." There are two things packed into that phrase that are easy to miss.

First, Paul's job was to bring the gospel to the Gentiles. "Gentiles" means everyone who isn't Jewish. For most of Israel's history, God had worked primarily through one nation. But the gospel broke that wide open. God's plan had always been to bless the whole world through Abraham's descendants, and now that plan was being fulfilled. Paul was the man God chose to carry the message beyond Israel's borders.

Second, notice what Paul says the gospel is supposed to produce: "the obedience that comes from faith." That phrase is important because it shows up at both the beginning and the end of Romans, like bookends holding the whole letter together. Paul isn't asking people to just believe something in their heads. Real faith changes how you live. It produces obedience, not the grudging, fearful kind, but the willing, joyful kind that flows out of trust. Faith and obedience aren't opposites. They're partners.

Paul then tells the Roman Christians something personal. He thanks God for them because their faith "is being reported all over the world." He has been praying for them constantly. He has longed to visit them for years.

Why does he want to come so badly? He gives several reasons. He wants to share some spiritual gift that will strengthen them. He wants to be mutually encouraged by their faith and theirs by his. He wants to "have a harvest" among them, meaning he wants to see people come to faith and grow in Christ.

Then Paul makes a statement that reveals his heart: "I am obligated both to Greeks and non-Greeks, both to the wise and the foolish." The word "obligated" means he's a debtor. Not because he borrowed something, but because he was entrusted with something. Jesus gave him the gospel to deliver, and until he delivers it, he owes a debt. It's like someone handing you a gift to pass along to a friend. Until you hand it over, you're carrying something that doesn't belong to you.

That's why Paul says, "I am so eager to preach the gospel also to you who are in Rome."

NOT ASHAMED

And then Paul makes the statement that launches the rest of the letter: "For I am not ashamed of the gospel, because it is the power of God that brings salvation to everyone who believes: first to the Jew, then to the Gentile."

Think about what Paul is saying here. He's writing to people who live in Rome, the capital of the most powerful empire the world had ever seen. Rome had armies, wealth, engineering, law, culture. It was the center of everything that mattered in the ancient world. And Paul is saying, "I have something more powerful than all of it."

Not a bigger army. Not a better political system. The gospel. A message about a Jewish carpenter who was executed by Rome and then came back from the dead.

Why would anyone not be ashamed of that? Because of what it does. The gospel is "the power of God that brings salvation." It doesn't just inform you. It rescues you. It doesn't just give you good advice. It unleashes the power of God to save people from sin, from death, from the wrath they deserve, and to bring them into a relationship with their Creator.

And this salvation is available to "everyone who believes." Not just the smart. Not just the religious. Not just the morally impressive. Everyone. The only requirement is faith: trusting that what God did through Jesus is enough.

Paul adds an important note: "first to the Jew, then to the Gentile." This isn't favoritism. It's history. God chose Israel to be the people through whom the Messiah would come. Jesus was Jewish. The first disciples were Jewish. The gospel went to the Jewish community first because that's where the story had been building for centuries. But it didn't stop there. It was always meant for the whole world.

THE HEART OF EVERYTHING

Paul finishes his opening with one more sentence that contains the beating heart of everything he's about to say: "For in the gospel the righteousness of God is revealed, a righteousness that is by faith from first to last, just as it is written: 'The righteous will live by faith.'"

This verse changed the world. Literally.

About fifteen hundred years after Paul wrote it, a German monk named Martin Luther was tormented by the phrase "the righteousness of God." He understood it as God's perfect standard of justice, the standard by which God condemns sinners. And since Luther knew he was a sinner, the phrase terrified him. How could God's righteousness be good news? It sounded like a death sentence.

Then Luther realized what Paul actually meant. The "righteousness of God" isn't just a standard that condemns us. It's a gift that saves us. God doesn't just demand righteousness. He provides it. Through the death and resurrection of Jesus, God offers to count sinners as righteous, not because they earned it, but because Jesus paid the penalty for their sins. It's not your righteousness that saves you. It's his.

And how do you receive this gift? By faith. From first to last.

Paul wraps it up by quoting the Old Testament prophet Habakkuk: "The righteous will live by faith." Habakkuk wrote those words during a dark time in Israel's history, when enemies were closing in and God seemed silent. God's answer to Habakkuk was simple: trust me. The person who is right with God will live by trusting God, even when nothing makes sense.

Paul takes that ancient truth and lifts it to its highest meaning. The person who is made right with God through faith will live, truly live, forever. Not because they were good enough. Because they trusted the One who is.

That's the gospel in one sentence. That's the seed that the rest of Romans will grow into a forest.

WHAT THIS MEANS FOR US

First, the gospel is the most important message you will ever hear. It's not a set of religious tips for being a nicer person. It's the announcement that God has done something to rescue you that you could never do for yourself. Every other message in the world tells you to try harder, be better, earn your place. The gospel says God has already done the work. Your job is to trust him.

Second, everyone needs the gospel equally. Paul says it's for "everyone who believes." Rich and poor. Smart and average. Religious and irreligious. Nobody is too good to need it, and nobody is too far gone to receive it. The ground is level at the foot of the cross.

Third, real faith produces real change. Paul talks about "the obedience that comes from faith." Believing in Jesus isn't just agreeing that certain facts are true. It means trusting him enough to follow him, to let his priorities become your priorities, to let his word shape how you live. Faith that doesn't change anything probably isn't faith at all.

Fourth, you don't have to be ashamed of the gospel. The world might think it's foolish. A crucified savior doesn't fit the world's idea of power. But Paul knew from personal experience that the gospel has the power to transform lives, communities, and entire civilizations. You're not carrying a weakness when you carry the gospel. You're carrying dynamite.

TALKING POINTS

1. **Paul described himself as a "slave" of Jesus Christ. Most people today resist the idea of belonging completely**

to anyone or anything. Why do you think Paul embraced that identity so willingly? What would it look like for someone your age to consider themselves completely devoted to Jesus?

2. **Paul says the gospel was "promised beforehand" in the Old Testament.** Why do you think it matters that God's plan wasn't a last-minute decision but something he had been preparing for centuries? How does that affect the way you trust him with your own life?

3. **Paul told the Romans he was "not ashamed of the gospel," even though preaching it in Rome could have seemed foolish or dangerous.** Have you ever felt pressure to keep quiet about what you believe? What made it hard, and what helped you through it?

4. **The phrase "the obedience that comes from faith" suggests that real belief and real action go together.** Can you think of an example where trusting someone naturally led to doing what they said? How does that help explain the connection between faith and obedience?

5. **Paul says the gospel reveals "the righteousness of God" as a gift received by faith.** Why do you think people sometimes struggle with the idea that they can't earn God's acceptance? What makes it hard to receive something you didn't work for?

Everything Paul has said so far is the headline. Now he's going to show us why we need this gospel so desperately. The answer isn't pretty, but it's honest.

Turn the page.

2

THE VERDICT NO ONE WANTS TO HEAR

The movie *Holes* starts with a kid named Stanley Yelnats getting arrested for something he didn't do. He's sent to Camp Green Lake, a juvenile detention center in the middle of a dried-up Texas desert, where the boys spend every day digging holes in the baking sun. The warden claims it "builds character." It doesn't take long to realize she's looking for something buried out there.

But here's what makes the movie so interesting. As the story unfolds, you learn that nearly every character is connected to a web of guilt that stretches back over a hundred years. The warden is guilty. The counselors are guilty. Stanley's no-good-dirty-rotten-pig-stealing great-great-grandfather set off a chain of events that cursed the whole family. Even the boys digging holes have their own stories of how they ended up there. Layer after layer, the film peels back and reveals that nobody's hands are clean. Everybody in this story is tangled up in the mess.

That's exactly what Paul does in Romans 1:18–3:20. He gathers the entire human race together and examines us so thoroughly that by the end, nobody has anything left to say. Not the obviously immoral person. Not the quietly judgmental person. Not even the deeply religious person. Every excuse falls apart. Every defense crumbles.

It's the hardest section of Romans to read. It's also the most necessary. Because you can't understand how good the good news is until you understand how bad the bad news is.

WHY BAD NEWS COMES FIRST

Think about it this way. If you go to a doctor and she tells you she has a cure for your disease, that's wonderful. But it only means something if you actually have the disease. If you think you're perfectly healthy, you'll shrug and walk away. The cure is wasted on someone who doesn't believe they're sick.

Paul has just finished telling us about the gospel, the most powerful rescue operation in history. God's righteousness has been revealed. Salvation is available to everyone who believes. But before Paul can explain how the rescue works, he has to prove that we need rescuing.

And he doesn't do it gently. He does it like a prosecutor laying out evidence, piece by piece, witness by witness, until the jury has no choice but to deliver a guilty verdict.

Paul divides humanity into groups and takes them one at a time. First, the obviously ungodly. Then, the self-righteous moralizers. Then, the religiously confident. And finally, every single person who has ever lived.

Nobody gets out clean.

THE WORLD THAT REJECTED GOD

Paul starts with the broadest and most visible category of sin: the open rebellion of people who knew God and turned away from him. "The wrath of God is being revealed from heaven against all the godlessness and wickedness of people, who suppress the truth by their wickedness."

Stop on that word "suppress." It doesn't mean they never had the truth. It means they did have it and shoved it down. Like someone holding a beach ball underwater. The truth keeps trying to surface, and they keep pushing it back under.

What truth? Paul explains: ever since the creation of the world, God's invisible qualities—his eternal power and divine nature—have been clearly seen through what he has made. In other words, creation itself is a billboard for God's existence. The stars, the mountains, the oceans, the staggering complexity of a single living cell. All of it points to a Creator. Nobody who has ever looked at the night sky with honest eyes can seriously say, "There's nothing behind all this."

Paul's conclusion is blunt: "so that people are without excuse."

Not without information. Without excuse. They had enough knowledge to respond to God, and they chose not to. Instead of worshiping the Creator, they worshiped created things. They traded the real God for substitutes: idols shaped like people, birds, animals, and reptiles.

In the ancient world, that meant literal statues in temples. In our world, it might look different. An idol is anything you treat as ultimate, anything you build your identity and happiness around that isn't God. Money. Popularity. Success. Your appearance. Your social media following. The shape of the idol changes from century to century. The impulse behind it never does.

And then Paul describes what happens when people push

God out of their lives. Three times he uses a terrifying phrase: "God gave them over."

God gave them over to impurity. God gave them over to shameful desires. God gave them over to a depraved mind.

This is what the wrath of God looks like in the present. It's not lightning bolts from the sky. It's God stepping back and letting people experience the consequences of their own choices. When you insist on running away from the only source of light, you end up in the dark. When you reject the one who designed you, you start to malfunction. That's not God being cruel. That's God honoring the choice you made, and letting you see where it leads.

Paul then lists the kinds of behavior that result: envy, murder, strife, deceit, malice, gossip, slander, arrogance, disobedience to parents, faithlessness, heartlessness, ruthlessness. It's a devastating catalog. And notice that it mixes things we'd consider extreme (murder) with things we might consider minor (gossip, envy). Paul doesn't rank sins the way we do. In God's courtroom, the whole list is evidence of the same disease.

The section ends with a chilling observation: the people who do these things know that they deserve judgment. And yet they not only keep doing them, they cheer on others who do the same.

If this were the whole story, it would be easy for the reader to sit back and think, "Well, that's about those people. The really bad ones. Not me."

Paul knows you're thinking that. And he's about to turn the spotlight directly on you.

THE JUDGE WHO'S ALSO GUILTY

"You, therefore, have no excuse, you who pass judgment on someone else, for at whatever point you judge another, you are condemning yourself, because you who pass judgment do the same things."

Paul has just described the openly sinful world, and he knows that some of his readers are nodding along. "Yes, Paul, those people are terrible. Thank goodness I'm not like them." This is the person who considers themselves morally superior. They might be a philosopher in Athens or a Sunday school teacher in your hometown. They see the mess other people make of their lives and feel a comfortable sense of distance.

But Paul says the moralist is guilty of the same things. Not necessarily the identical actions, but the same fundamental problem: they know what's right and still don't do it consistently. The difference between the openly rebellious person and the quietly judgmental person isn't innocence. It's hypocrisy. One does wrong and doesn't care. The other does wrong and pretends not to.

Paul asks a devastating question: "Do you think you will escape God's judgment?" You who criticize everyone else, do you really think God won't notice that you're doing the very things you condemn?

Then Paul addresses something people do when they sense they might be in trouble with God. They point to his kindness and patience and say, "See? God hasn't punished me. He must not mind." But Paul says God's kindness isn't approval. It's an invitation. His patience is meant to lead you toward repentance, toward a genuine change of heart and direction.

Mistaking God's patience for permission is one of the most dangerous mistakes a person can make.

Paul then lays out a principle that applies to everyone: God will judge each person according to what they have done. Those who persistently seek glory, honor, and immortality by doing good will receive eternal life. Those who are self-seeking, who reject the truth and follow evil, will experience God's wrath. And this applies equally. "First for the Jew, then for the Gentile." God does not play favorites.

But what about people who never had the Bible? What about those who never heard God's law read out loud in a synagogue or a church?

Paul has an answer for that too. Even people who don't have God's written law still have a sense of right and wrong written on their hearts. Their consciences bear witness, sometimes accusing them, sometimes defending them. They may not have the Ten Commandments carved in stone, but they have a moral awareness built into their humanity. And they've violated even that.

No one can claim total ignorance. Everyone has enough moral knowledge to be held accountable.

WHEN RELIGION ISN'T ENOUGH

Now Paul turns to the group that might seem the safest of all: the Jewish people, God's chosen nation.

Remember, Paul himself was Jewish. He wasn't attacking his own people out of hostility. He was dismantling a dangerous assumption that many of them carried: the belief that being Jewish, possessing God's law, and bearing the sign of circumcision automatically made them right with God.

Paul doesn't deny that the Jewish people had tremendous privileges. God really did choose them. He really did entrust them with his word. He really did make a covenant with them. Those things mattered. But Paul insists that privilege brings responsibility, not immunity.

"You who brag about the law, do you dishonor God by breaking the law?"

He fires off a series of uncomfortable questions. You teach others not to steal, but do you steal? You say people shouldn't commit adultery, but do you? You claim to hate idols, but do you rob temples? The details may vary, but the point is unmistakable: knowing God's standards and keeping God's standards are two very different things.

This is where Paul says something that would have stunned his Jewish readers. Circumcision, the physical sign that marked every Jewish male as part of God's covenant people, has value only if you obey the law. If you break the law, your circumcision means nothing. And if an uncircumcised Gentile actually keeps the law's requirements, that person will be counted as though they were circumcised.

In other words, what God cares about is the heart, not the ceremony. A real member of God's people isn't defined by an outward mark but by an inward reality. True circumcision is "of the heart, by the Spirit."

This principle applies far beyond first-century Judaism. It applies to anyone who trusts in religious rituals, church attendance, baptism certificates, or family heritage as proof that they're right with God. Those things may be meaningful. But none of them substitute for a heart that actually trusts and obeys God.

Paul then anticipates the obvious pushback. If being Jewish doesn't automatically save you, then what's the point of being Jewish at all? His answer: the Jews were given an enormous privilege. They were entrusted with the very words of God. That's not nothing. But privilege doesn't guarantee faithfulness. Some Jews believed, and some didn't. And God's faithfulness to his promises is not cancelled by human unfaithfulness.

But does God's faithfulness mean he won't judge his own people? Absolutely not. God is the judge of the whole world, and his judgment must be fair. You can't argue that your sin somehow glorifies God by making his grace look better, so he shouldn't punish you. Paul calls that reasoning what it is: absurd.

EVERY MOUTH SILENCED

Now Paul delivers the closing argument. He's gone through the openly immoral, the quietly judgmental, and the religiously confident. He's shown that each group had knowledge of God and goodness, and each group failed to live up to what they knew. Now he gathers all of humanity together and delivers the verdict.

"What shall we conclude then? Do we have any advantage? Not at all! For we have already made the charge that Jews and Gentiles alike are all under the power of sin."

Then Paul does something a rabbi would recognize immediately. He strings together a chain of Old Testament quotations, one after another, like a prosecutor reading off a list of charges:

"There is no one righteous, not even one; there is no one who understands; there is no one who seeks God. All have turned away, they have together become worthless; there is no one who does good, not even one."

"Their throats are open graves; their tongues practice deceit." "The poison of vipers is on their lips." "Their mouths are full of cursing and bitterness." "Their feet are swift to shed blood; ruin and misery mark their ways, and the way of peace they do not know." "There is no fear of God before their eyes."

Read those slowly. Notice what Paul is doing. He's working through the human body, part by part. Throats. Tongues. Lips. Mouths. Feet. Eyes. Every part of us has been recruited into the rebellion. Sin isn't just something we do occasionally. It has infected every dimension of who we are: our speech, our actions, our vision, our direction.

This doesn't mean every person is as bad as they could possibly be. Clearly, people do kind and generous things every day. But it does mean that no part of us is untouched by sin. Even our best moments are mixed with selfish motives we'd rather not examine too closely.

And then comes the line that seals everything shut: "Therefore no one will be declared righteous in God's sight by the works of the law; rather, through the law we become conscious of our sin."

The law was never designed to save you. It was designed to show you that you need saving. It's like a mirror. A mirror can show you that your face is dirty, but you can't wash your face with a mirror. The law diagnoses the disease. It doesn't provide the cure.

Paul has done what he set out to do. Every mouth is silenced. The whole world stands accountable to God. Not because God is harsh, but because he is honest. And honest diagnosis is the only path to real healing.

WHAT THIS MEANS FOR US

First, every human being needs the gospel. Not just "bad" people. Not just people who have committed dramatic sins. Everyone. The person who goes to church every Sunday needs the gospel just as much as the person who has never set foot in one. There are no exceptions to the human problem, which means there are no exceptions to the need for a divine solution.

Second, judging others doesn't make you innocent. It's easy to look at someone else's failures and feel better about yourself. Paul says that instinct is a trap. The moment you set yourself up as judge over someone else, you've proven that you know the standard, which means you're accountable to it too. Compassion, not condemnation, is the proper response to other people's sin, because we share the same disease.

Third, religious activity can't replace a changed heart. Knowing the Bible, attending church, and being baptized are important, but they're not substitutes for genuine trust in God and a life that reflects that trust. God isn't impressed by the outward performance if the inward reality doesn't match.

Fourth, the law is a gift, even when it hurts. Being told the truth about yourself is uncomfortable. But it's the only way forward. A doctor who refuses to tell you about a serious diagnosis isn't being kind. He's being negligent. God's law tells us the truth about our condition so that we'll stop trying to cure ourselves and start looking for the real physician.

TALKING POINTS

1. **Paul says that people "suppress the truth" about God even though creation makes his existence plain.** Why do you think people resist acknowledging God even when the evidence is all around them? Have you ever experienced that tension yourself?

2. **Three times in this passage, Paul says "God gave them over."** What does it tell you about God that his judgment sometimes looks like simply letting people have what they want? Why might that be the most frightening kind of judgment?

3. **Paul says the person who judges others is guilty of the same things. That doesn't mean the same exact actions, but the same core problem.** Why do you think it's so tempting to focus on other people's sins instead of our own? What would change if we were as honest about ourselves as we are about others?

4. **The Jewish people had real, God-given privileges, but Paul says those privileges didn't make them immune to judgment.** Can you think of ways that Christians today might make a similar mistake, trusting in their religious identity rather than in God himself?

5. **Paul says the purpose of the law is not to save us but to show us our sin.** How does that change the way you think about God's commands? If the law is like a mirror, what is the "soap" that actually makes us clean?

The courtroom is silent. The evidence is in. Every person on earth stands guilty, and no one has a defense. If the story ended here, it would be the most hopeless moment in all of Scripture.

But the story doesn't end here. Not even close.

Turn the page.

3

THE GIFT NO ONE EARNED

Have you ever gotten something you knew you didn't deserve? Maybe you bombed a test, and the teacher offered extra credit that saved your grade. Maybe you broke something at a friend's house, and their parent said, "Don't worry about it. It's taken care of." Maybe you were the last kid picked for a team, and then someone traded spots so you could play.

There's a strange feeling that comes with a gift like that. Part of you is relieved. Part of you is grateful. And part of you isn't sure whether to accept it because you know, deep down, that you didn't earn it. You know the score. You know what you deserved. And what you got instead doesn't match up.

Now multiply that feeling by infinity. Because what Paul is about to describe in Romans 3:21 is the moment when God looked at a guilty world—a world he had just finished proving was completely without excuse—and instead of delivering the punishment everyone deserved, he offered a gift so enormous that people are still struggling to accept it two thousand years later.

Two words signal the turn in Paul's argument: "But now." Those might be the two most important words in the entire letter.

THE TURN

"But now apart from the law the righteousness of God has been made known, to which the Law and the Prophets testify."

Do you feel the shift? Everything before this was darkness. Every mouth silenced. The whole world guilty. No one righteous, not even one. If the letter ended at Romans 3:20, it would be the most depressing document ever written.

But now.

Something has happened. Something has changed. God has acted. And what he has done changes everything for everyone.

Paul says that "the righteousness of God" has been made known. We talked about this phrase back in chapter 1, where Paul first introduced it. Now he's returning to it with the full weight of the bad news behind him. Remember, the problem isn't just that people have done bad things. The problem is that people are unable to make themselves right with God through their own efforts. The law can show you what's wrong, but it can't fix you. It's a mirror, not soap.

So God did what we could never do. He provided a righteousness that doesn't come from our performance. It comes from him.

And here's the key: this righteousness "comes through faith in Jesus Christ to all who believe."

Not to all who earn it. Not to all who deserve it. Not to all who follow enough rules, attend enough services, or impress enough people. To all who believe.

Paul immediately explains why this offer is universal: "There is no difference between Jew and Gentile, for all have sinned and fall short of the glory of God."

That phrase, "fall short of the glory of God," is worth pausing on. God created human beings to reflect his glory, the way the moon reflects the light of the sun. We were designed to mirror his goodness, his beauty, his character. But sin bent the mirror. Every person, no matter how moral or religious, falls short of what we were made to be. The gap between us and God's glory isn't something we can bridge by trying harder. We need someone to bridge it for us.

THREE PICTURES OF RESCUE

Paul then packs three enormous ideas into just two verses. Each one is a different picture of what God did through Jesus.

The first picture is justification. Paul says we "are justified freely by his grace." Justification is a courtroom word. It means to be declared "not guilty," to be pronounced righteous by the judge. But here's what makes it astonishing: the people being declared righteous are actually guilty. God isn't pretending they didn't sin. He's saying that the penalty for their sin has been paid by someone else. The verdict is real because the payment is real.

And it's free. Paul uses that word deliberately. You don't earn a verdict of "not guilty" when someone else pays your fine. You receive it.

The second picture is redemption. Paul says justification comes "through the redemption that came by Christ Jesus." Redemption is a slavery word. In the ancient world, a slave could be set free if someone paid the price to buy their freedom. That's what God did. We were enslaved to sin, unable to free ourselves, and Jesus paid the ransom. His death was the price of our liberation.

The third picture is sacrifice. Paul says that "God presented Christ as a sacrifice of atonement, through the shedding of his blood." This takes us back to the Old Testament, where once a year, on the Day of Atonement, the high priest would sprinkle blood on the cover of the ark of the covenant to make things right between God and his sinful people. The sacrificial system was always pointing forward to something bigger. Jesus is that something bigger. His death on the cross is the ultimate sacrifice, the one that actually deals with sin once and for all.

Notice who takes the initiative in all three pictures. God does. God declares us righteous. God pays the ransom. God provides the sacrifice. Salvation isn't something we achieve. It's something God accomplishes and then offers to us as a gift.

And how do we receive this gift? By faith. We trust that what God did through Jesus is enough. We stop trying to earn our way into his favor and start resting in what he has already done.

WHY GOD DID IT THIS WAY

Paul then explains why the cross was necessary. It wasn't just about saving us. It was about showing that God is just.

Here's the problem God was solving. For centuries, God had been patient with sin. He didn't destroy every sinner the moment they sinned. He showed mercy and patience over and over again. But that raises a question: Was God just looking the other way? Was he too soft on sin? Did he not care about justice?

The cross answers that question with a thunderclap. At the cross, God demonstrated that he takes sin with absolute seriousness. The penalty was paid in full, not by the sinner, but by his own Son. Justice was satisfied. Mercy was extended.

And God proved that he is both "just and the one who justifies those who have faith in Jesus."

Both at the same time. That's the miracle of the cross. God didn't choose between being fair and being merciful. He found a way to be both.

NO ROOM FOR BOASTING

After laying all this out, Paul asks a simple question: "Where, then, is boasting?"

His answer: it's been eliminated. Shut out. Gone.

If salvation came through keeping the law, through being good enough, through earning God's approval, then the people who pulled it off could brag about it. But salvation comes through faith. And faith, by definition, is admitting that you can't do it yourself. You can't boast about receiving a gift. You can only be grateful.

This also means that God isn't the God of one group only. He's not just the God of the Jewish people, and he's not just the God of the religious people. He is the God of everyone, and he justifies everyone the same way: through faith. Circumcision or not. Law or no law. The ground is level. Nobody gets special treatment, and nobody gets left out.

EXHIBIT A: ABRAHAM

At this point, Paul knows his Jewish readers are thinking, "That sounds nice, Paul, but what about Abraham? Our father Abraham was righteous because of what he did. He obeyed God. He left his homeland. He offered up his own son Isaac. Surely he earned his standing with God."

Paul's answer is devastating in its simplicity. He quotes Genesis 15:6: "Abraham believed God, and it was credited to him as righteousness."

Read that carefully. Abraham believed. And God credited it, counted it, reckoned it to him as righteousness. Abraham didn't earn righteousness through a lifetime of good works. He received it through faith. God made a promise, Abraham trusted the promise, and God declared him righteous on the basis of that trust.

Paul then uses an illustration anyone can understand. When you work a job, your paycheck isn't a gift. It's something you earned. Your employer owes it to you. But when you don't work and instead trust the God "who justifies the ungodly," your faith is credited as righteousness. It's a gift, not a wage.

Did you catch that phrase? God justifies the ungodly. Not the godly. Not the well-behaved. Not the people who have it all together. The ungodly. That's the most shocking thing Paul has said yet. The God of the universe specializes in declaring guilty people righteous, not because they cleaned themselves up first, but because they trusted him to do what they couldn't.

Paul backs this up with King David, who wrote in Psalm 32: "Blessed are those whose transgressions are forgiven, whose sins are covered. Blessed is the one whose sin the Lord will never count against them." David knew what it was like to be forgiven. He had committed adultery and murder. He was not a man who could boast about his moral record. But God forgave him anyway. And David called that the greatest blessing a person could ever receive.

BEFORE THE SURGERY, NOT AFTER

Then Paul asks a question that might seem technical but carries enormous weight: when was Abraham credited with righteousness? Was it before he was circumcised, or after?

The answer: before. By a long stretch. Genesis 15, where Abraham is declared righteous by faith, comes well before Genesis 17, where he receives circumcision. That means Abraham's right standing with God had nothing to do with the religious ritual that would later mark Israel as God's people.

Why does this matter? Because it means Abraham is the father of everyone who believes, not just the Jewish people. He received righteousness by faith while he was still, technically, an outsider. No circumcision. No law of Moses. Nothing but a promise from God and the faith to trust it.

Circumcision came later, and Paul says it was "a sign, a seal" of the righteousness Abraham already had. It confirmed what faith had already accomplished. It didn't create it.

This is Paul's way of saying that no religious ritual, however meaningful, can substitute for faith. Living obediently matters. Church participation matters. But none of those things create your right standing with God. Faith does. The rituals confirm and express what faith has already received.

WHAT ABRAHAM ACTUALLY BELIEVED

Paul wraps up the chapter by describing what Abraham's faith looked like in practice. And it wasn't easy.

God promised Abraham that he would be "the father of many nations." But Abraham was nearly a hundred years old. His body was, as Paul puts it bluntly, "as good as dead." Sarah's womb was dead too. By every human measurement, the promise was impossible.

But Abraham didn't focus on the impossibility. He focused on the one who made the promise. "He did not waver through unbelief regarding the promise of God, but was strengthened in his faith and gave glory to God, being fully persuaded that God had power to do what he had promised."

That's what faith looks like. Not pretending the obstacles aren't real. Not ignoring the facts. But being more convinced of God's power than of the problem's size.

And then Paul lands the plane. He says the words "it was credited to him" weren't written just for Abraham. They were written "for us, to whom God will credit righteousness, for us who believe in him who raised Jesus our Lord from the dead."

Abraham believed God could bring life from a dead body. We believe God raised Jesus from a dead tomb. It's the same kind of faith, aimed at the same kind of God: the God who brings life out of death.

The final verse of the chapter says it all: "He was delivered over to death for our sins and was raised to life for our justification."

Jesus died because of what we did. Jesus rose so that we could be declared righteous. The cross paid the penalty. The resurrection proved the payment was accepted.

That's the gift no one earned. And it's yours for the taking.

WHAT THIS MEANS FOR US

First, salvation is a gift, and gifts change how you live. When someone gives you something you know you don't deserve, the natural response isn't laziness. It's gratitude. It's wanting to honor the giver. Grace doesn't make people careless. It makes them grateful, and gratitude is the strongest motivation for a changed life.

Second, faith is not a feeling. It's a decision to trust. Abraham didn't feel confident every day. He faced facts that should have crushed his hope. But he chose to trust the God who made the promise. Faith doesn't mean you never doubt. It means you trust God more than you trust your doubts.

Third, your past doesn't disqualify you. God justifies the ungodly. David was an adulterer and a murderer, and God called him blessed. Abraham was an old man with a barren wife, and God made him the father of nations. If God only worked with perfect people, he would work with nobody. Your failures are real, but God's grace is bigger.

Fourth, no ritual replaces real faith. Circumcision didn't save Abraham. Living obediently doesn't save you in and of itself. Church attendance doesn't save you. These things matter because they express and confirm what God has done in your heart. But the heart is where it starts. God looks at the inside.

TALKING POINTS

1. **Paul says that God is both "just" and "the one who justifies" through the cross.** Why is it important that God didn't simply ignore sin but actually dealt with it? What would it mean if God just looked the other way?

2. **Paul uses three pictures for what God did through Jesus: justification (a courtroom), redemption (a slave market), and sacrifice (a temple).** Which of those pictures helps you understand the gospel best, and why?

3. **Abraham was declared righteous before he was circumcised, which means the religious ritual came after the relationship with God, not before it.** How might this change the way people think about religious activities like church attendance, baptism, or Bible reading?

4. **Paul says Abraham was "fully persuaded that God had power to do what he had promised," even when the circumstances seemed impossible.** Can you think of a time when trusting someone required you to believe something that seemed unlikely? What made you decide to trust?

5. **The chapter ends by saying Jesus "was delivered over to death for our sins and was raised to life for our justification."** Why do you think both the death and the resurrection are necessary? What would be missing if only one of them happened?

The verdict has been overturned. The guilty have been declared righteous. The slaves have been set free. But what does this new life actually look like? What changes when you go from being an enemy of God to being at peace with him?

Turn the page.

4

PEACE WITH GOD

There's a moment near the end of *The Iron Giant* that changes everything. A massive nuclear missile is hurtling toward the small town of Rockwell, Maine. There's no way to stop it. Everyone is going to die.

And then the Giant, the alien robot who has spent the whole movie learning what it means to be alive, makes a choice. He flies straight at the missile. His friend Hogarth screams for him to come back, but the Giant keeps going. He closes his eyes, whispers "Superman," and collides with the missile in the upper atmosphere. The explosion lights up the sky. The town is saved. The Giant is gone.

One sacrifice. One act. And it changed everything for everyone below.

Romans 5 is the chapter where Paul shows us what Christ's sacrifice actually accomplished. He has already proven that everyone is guilty. He has already explained that God offers righteousness as a gift through faith. Now he answers the question that logically comes next: what does this gift actually do? What changes when you go from being guilty to being justified?

The answer is bigger than you might expect. It's not just about you and your personal forgiveness. It's about the entire human race, two men who stand at the crossroads of history, and a grace so massive it makes the worst disaster in human history look small by comparison.

WHAT JUSTIFIED PEOPLE HAVE

Paul opens the chapter with a string of statements that read almost like a list of treasures being placed into your hands, one after another. "Therefore, since we have been justified through faith, we have peace with God through our Lord Jesus Christ."

Peace with God. Not just a calm feeling. Not just the absence of stress. This is the end of a war. Before justification, every human being was in a state of hostility with God. We were rebels against his authority, violators of his law, and objects of his righteous anger. Justification doesn't just forgive the crimes. It ends the conflict. The war is over. The relationship is restored.

And notice how it happened: "through our Lord Jesus Christ." Jesus is the peacemaker. He is the one who stood between a holy God and a sinful humanity and made reconciliation possible.

But peace is only the beginning. Paul says that through Jesus "we have gained access by faith into this grace in which we now stand." Picture a throne room. Before justification, the door was locked. You had no right to enter. But Jesus opened the door and brought you in. Now you're standing in the presence of the King, not as a criminal awaiting sentencing, but as a welcomed guest. And you're standing in grace. Grace isn't something you visited once. It's the ground under your feet. It's where you live now.

Then Paul adds something that might surprise you: "And we boast in the hope of the glory of God."

Remember how Paul said in the last chapter that boasting is eliminated? He meant boasting in yourself, in your own achievements, in your own righteousness. That kind of boasting is dead. But there's a completely different kind of boasting that justified people do: they boast in what God is going to do. They look forward with confident joy to the day when God's glory will be fully revealed and they will share in it. The same glory that humanity "fell short of" back in Romans 3:23, justified people will one day receive in full.

Peace with God. Access to grace. Hope of glory. That's what justification gives you.

THE STRANGE LOGIC OF SUFFERING

Then Paul says something that nobody expected: "Not only so, but we also glory in our sufferings."

Wait. Suffering? We just got peace and grace and hope. Now suffering?

Paul isn't saying Christians enjoy pain. He's not promoting some twisted idea that hurting is good for its own sake. He's saying something far more practical: suffering, when you go through it with faith, produces something valuable that you can't get any other way.

Here's the chain: suffering produces perseverance. Perseverance produces character. Character produces hope. And hope does not put us to shame.

Think of it like a chain reaction. When you face hardship and don't give up, you develop endurance. When you've endured and come out the other side, you develop a tested, proven character, the kind of character that can only be forged under pressure. And when you have that kind of character, you develop a deeper, more resilient hope, because you've seen God sustain you through things you didn't think you could survive.

This isn't wishful thinking. Paul says this hope is reliable because "God's love has been poured out into our hearts through the Holy Spirit, who has been given to us." The ultimate proof that your hope is well-placed isn't your own track record. It's God's love, actively poured into you by his Spirit. You can trust the hope because you can trust the one who gave it to you.

THE PROOF OF LOVE

Then Paul makes the case for God's love in the most dramatic way possible. "You see, at just the right time, when we were still powerless, Christ died for the ungodly."

Catch those words. Not for the deserving. Not for the impressive. For the ungodly. For the powerless. For people who had absolutely nothing to offer him.

Paul puts it in perspective: "Very rarely will anyone die for a righteous person, though for a good person someone might possibly dare to die." In other words, human love has limits. You might sacrifice yourself for a genuinely good person, someone noble, someone worth it. But even that is extremely rare.

"But God demonstrates his own love for us in this: while we were still sinners, Christ died for us."

That's the proof. Not words about love. Not feelings about love. An action. A death. And the timing matters as much as the act itself. God didn't wait until we cleaned up our lives. He didn't wait until we showed some potential. He loved us at our absolute worst. While we were still sinners. While we were still his enemies. That is the measure of divine love. It doesn't respond to our worthiness. It creates worth where there was none.

SAVED FROM WHAT'S COMING

Paul now shifts from past to future. If God already did the hardest thing (saving us while we were enemies), then everything that comes next is guaranteed.

"Since we have now been justified by his blood, how much more shall we be saved from God's wrath through him!"

This is what theologians call an "argument from the greater to the lesser." If God loved you enough to send his Son to die for you when you were his enemy, he certainly won't abandon you now that you're his friend. If the cross happened when the relationship was at its worst, how much more will God protect and preserve you now that the relationship has been restored?

Paul puts it another way: "If, when we were God's enemies, we were reconciled to him through the death of his Son, how much more, having been reconciled, shall we be saved through his life!"

Two words matter here. Reconciled and saved. Reconciliation has already happened through the cross. But there is a future dimension to salvation that hasn't been completed yet. One day, God's wrath will fall on the unrepentant world, and those who belong to Christ will be delivered completely. One day, Christians will receive new bodies in a new creation. The cross secured the relationship. The resurrection guarantees the future.

Paul closes this section by saying that we "boast in God through our Lord Jesus Christ, through whom we have now received reconciliation." Christian boasting isn't pride. It's pure gratitude directed at the one who did everything for us when we could do nothing for ourselves.

TWO MEN, TWO WORLDS

Now Paul does something breathtaking. He zooms all the way out, past your individual life, past even the history of Israel, to the very beginning of the human story. He places two men side by side: Adam and Christ. And he shows that the entire history of the human race can be understood through what these two men did.

"Therefore, just as sin entered the world through one man, and death through sin, and in this way death came to all people, because all sinned..."

Adam's one act of disobedience opened the door to sin. And sin brought death. Not just physical death, but spiritual separation from God. And this death spread to every single person who ever lived. Nobody escapes Adam's legacy. We are all born into a world already broken by his choice.

Paul acknowledges that sin existed in the world even before the law of Moses was given. People were sinning and dying long before God handed down the Ten Commandments at Mount Sinai. The law didn't create the problem. It revealed and defined the problem that was already there.

But Adam, Paul says, "is a pattern of the one to come." Adam was a preview of Christ, but an opposite kind of preview. Both are heads of a whole humanity. Both changed the destiny of everyone connected to them. But where Adam brought disaster, Christ brought rescue.

THE GIFT IS NOT LIKE THE TRESPASS

Paul spends the rest of the chapter hammering home one point: what Christ did is far greater than what Adam did. The two are not equal. Grace doesn't just match the damage of sin. It overwhelms it.

"But the gift is not like the trespass. For if the many died by the trespass of the one man, how much more did God's grace and the gift that came by the grace of the one man, Jesus Christ, overflow to the many!"

One man sinned, and millions died. But one man obeyed, and God's grace overflowed. Notice the language Paul keeps using: "how much more." Grace isn't playing catch-up with sin. It's running laps around it.

Paul draws the contrast in three ways. First, Adam's one trespass brought condemnation, but Christ's one act of righteousness brought justification. Second, through Adam's disobedience, the many were made sinners; through Christ's obedience, the many will be made righteous. Third, through Adam, death reigned like a tyrant over the human race. But through Christ, those who receive grace will themselves reign in life.

Did you catch that last one? It doesn't say that life will reign over them, as though they simply traded one king for a nicer one. It says they will reign. People who were slaves to death become kings in life. That's not just a change of circumstances. It's a complete reversal of identity.

Then Paul adds one of the most stunning sentences in the entire Bible: "Where sin increased, grace increased all the more."

Sin is powerful. It has wrecked individuals, families, nations, and civilizations. But grace is more powerful still. For every sin that has ever been committed, God's grace rises higher. There is no depth of human evil that God's grace cannot reach, no sin so enormous that his mercy cannot cover it.

And the whole thing ends with a purpose statement: "so that, just as sin reigned in death, so also grace might reign through righteousness to bring eternal life through Jesus Christ our Lord."

Two kingdoms. Two reigns. Sin reigned, and its currency was death. Grace reigns, and its currency is eternal life. And the bridge between the two kingdoms is Jesus Christ.

WHAT THIS MEANS FOR US

First, peace with God changes everything else. When the most important relationship in your life is settled, everything else falls into perspective. Troubles at school, conflicts with friends, uncertainty about the future: none of those go away, but they all look different when you know that the God of the universe is no longer against you but for you.

Second, suffering is not wasted. That doesn't make it fun, and it doesn't mean you should go looking for it. But when hard things come, and they will, you can face them knowing that God uses pressure to build something in you that comfort never could. Perseverance, character, and hope are forged in difficulty, not in ease.

Third, God's love is proven, not promised. Lots of people will tell you they love you. God showed you. He sent his Son to die for you while you were still his enemy. That's not a theory. It's history. And it means you never have to wonder whether God really cares.

Fourth, you are part of a bigger story. Your life isn't just about you. You are connected to Adam, and through faith, you are connected to Christ. The choices of these two men ripple through all of human history, and the one you belong to by faith determines your destiny. In Adam, death reigns. In Christ, you reign in life.

TALKING POINTS

1. **Paul says that suffering produces perseverance, perseverance produces character, and character produces hope.** Can you think of a time when going through something hard actually made you stronger or taught you something important? What did that experience look like?

2. **Paul writes that Christ died for us "while we were still sinners."** Why do you think the timing of God's love matters so much? How is it different from the way most people love?

3. **Paul compares Adam and Christ as two leaders whose actions affected everyone connected to them.** Why do you think God chose to work through representative people rather than dealing with every individual separately? Can you think of other examples where one person's decision affected an entire group?

4. **Paul says "where sin increased, grace increased all the more."** Does that mean people should keep sinning so grace keeps growing? Why or why not? (Hint: Paul will address this exact question in the next chapter.)

5. **The chapter ends with two competing "reigns": sin reigning in death and grace reigning in life.** What does it look like practically for someone your age to live under the reign of grace rather than the reign of sin?

Two men. Two choices. Two outcomes for the entire human race. But if grace really is more powerful than sin, if the gift really does overwhelm the trespass, then what stops someone from saying, "Great, I'll just keep sinning and let grace keep covering it"?

Paul heard that objection coming from a mile away.

Turn the page.

5

DEAD TO SIN

Early in Mark Twain's *Adventures of Huckleberry Finn*, Huck finds himself in a desperate situation. His violent, drunken father has kidnapped him and locked him in a cabin in the woods. There's no reasoning with the man and no one coming to help. So Huck hatches a plan. He kills a wild pig, smears the blood around the cabin, drags a bag of meal to the river, and stages the whole scene to look like a murder. Then he slips away in a canoe. As far as the world is concerned, Huckleberry Finn is dead.

But of course he isn't dead. He's more alive than ever. He's escaped. He's free. And as the story unfolds, Huck lives an entirely new life on the Mississippi River, a life his old self could never have imagined.

Here's the thing, though. Huck can never go back. He faked his own death. If he walks back into town and picks up where he left off, the whole escape becomes meaningless. His freedom depends on staying dead to his old life.

That's almost exactly the argument Paul makes in Romans 6. In the previous chapters, Paul has explained that God justifies sinners freely by his grace, that where sin increased, grace increased all the more. But that raises a question that Paul knows someone is going to ask. If grace gets bigger every time sin gets bigger, then why not just keep sinning? Wouldn't that make grace even more impressive?

Paul's answer is explosive. And it starts with a death.

THE QUESTION THAT HAD TO BE ASKED

"What shall we say, then? Shall we go on sinning so that grace may increase?" Paul isn't making this up. People were actually saying this about his teaching. Back in chapter 3, he mentioned that some were slandering him by claiming he taught "let us do evil that good may result." Now he deals with it head on.

His answer comes fast and hard: "By no means!"

That translation is polite. Paul's actual tone is closer to "Absolutely not!" or "That's unthinkable!" He is genuinely shocked that anyone could draw that conclusion from what he's been saying. And then he explains why.

"We are those who have died to sin; how can we live in it any longer?"

This is the key sentence of the whole chapter. Christians have died to sin. Not "are trying to die to sin." Not "hope to die to sin someday." Have died. Past tense. It's already happened. And if you're dead to something, you can't keep living in it. A dead person doesn't respond to the things that used to control them. The relationship is over.

But what does it mean to "die to sin"? Paul doesn't mean that Christians never sin again or that sin stops being tempting. He means something deeper and more specific. Through faith, repentance, and baptism, Christians have been united with Christ. And what happened to Christ happened to them. Christ died to pay the penalty for sin, once and for all. When you are joined to Christ by faith, repentance, and baptism, his death counts as your death. The penalty has been paid. Sin's legal claim on your life has been settled. You are, in the eyes of God's justice, dead to sin.

And Paul says the proof of this is your baptism.

BURIED AND RAISED

"Or don't you know that all of us who were baptized into Christ Jesus were baptized into his death? We were therefore buried with him through baptism into death, in order that, just as Christ was raised from the dead through the glory of the Father, we too may live a new life."

Baptism, for Paul, is not just a ritual or a ceremony. It's a dramatic reenactment of the gospel itself. When you go down into the water, you are picturing your death and burial with Christ. When you come up out of the water, you are picturing your resurrection with him. Baptism is like a door between two rooms. You walk through it, and the old room is behind you. You're in a new space now. A new life.

Paul isn't saying that the water itself saves you. He's been arguing for chapters that salvation comes through faith. But baptism is the moment when you identify yourself with Christ's death and resurrection. It's where you say, "I am done with the old life. I belong to Jesus now."

And the point Paul keeps driving home is this: if you have been buried with Christ and raised with him, then going back to your old life makes no sense. It would be like Huck Finn staging an elaborate death scene and then walking back into his father's cabin the next morning. The whole thing would be absurd.

THE OLD SELF, CRUCIFIED

Paul pushes the logic further. "For we know that our old self was crucified with him so that the body ruled by sin might be done away with, that we should no longer be slaves to sin, because anyone who has died has been set free from sin."

Your "old self" is the person you were before you came to faith, the person defined by sin, enslaved to it, unable to escape its grip. Paul says that old self was crucified with Christ. It was nailed to the cross alongside him. Not in some mystical, make-believe sense, but in the sense that Christ's death counts for you. His penalty covered yours. And because the penalty has been paid, sin no longer has the legal right to enslave you.

Think of it like a prisoner who has served their full sentence. When they walk out of prison, they are free. The law has no more claim on them. They've paid their debt. That's the position of every Christian. Through union with Christ, the debt has been paid. Sin's power isn't destroyed in the sense that it stops existing, but it is broken in the sense that it no longer owns you. You are no longer obligated to obey it.

Paul then makes the positive side of the argument: "Now if we died with Christ, we believe that we will also live with him. For we know that since Christ was raised from the dead, he cannot die again; death no longer has mastery over him."

Christ died once and will never die again. Death took its best shot, and Jesus walked out of the tomb. Death's power over him is permanently finished. And if you are united with Christ, the same is true for you. You share in his victory. The life you now live is resurrection life, life that has already passed through death and come out the other side.

COUNT YOURSELVES

So what are Christians supposed to do with all of this? Paul gives a simple, powerful instruction: "In the same way, count yourselves dead to sin but alive to God in Christ Jesus."

This isn't pretending. Paul isn't asking you to close your eyes and imagine really hard that sin doesn't tempt you anymore. He's asking you to remember what's already true. You have died to sin. You are alive to God. Now live like it. Think about your life from that reality instead of from the old one.

It's like the Duke of Windsor once said about his father, King George V, who used to tell him, "My dear boy, you must always remember who you are." That's Paul's message to every Christian. Remember who you are. You are not the person you used to be. You died with Christ. You rose with Christ. Act accordingly.

Then Paul gets practical. "Therefore do not let sin reign in your mortal body so that you obey its evil desires. Do not offer any part of yourself to sin as an instrument of wickedness, but rather offer yourselves to God as those who have been brought from death to life; and offer every part of yourself to him as an instrument of righteousness."

Your hands, your eyes, your mouth, your mind: every part of you can be used either as a tool for sin or as a tool for God. You get to choose which. Sin will try to reclaim the throne. It will whisper that it still owns you. But Paul says it doesn't. You are under grace, not under law, and grace doesn't give sin permission. Grace gives you the power to say no.

SWITCHING MASTERS

Halfway through the chapter, someone asks the question again, slightly rephrased: "What then? Shall we sin because we are not under the law but under grace?"

Paul gives the same answer: "By no means!"

Then he shifts the image. Instead of death and resurrection, he talks about slavery. "Don't you know that when you offer yourselves to someone as obedient slaves, you are slaves of the one you obey, whether you are slaves to sin, which leads to death, or to obedience, which leads to righteousness?"

Everyone serves something. That's Paul's point. There's no such thing as total freedom in the sense of answering to nothing and no one. You're either a slave to sin or a slave to God. Those are the only two options. And the two slaveries lead to completely different destinations. Sin pays in death. God gives the gift of life.

Paul thanks God that although his readers "used to be slaves to sin," they "have come to obey from your heart the pattern of teaching that has now claimed your allegiance." Notice the phrase "from your heart." This isn't forced obedience. It isn't grudging rule-following. It's a willing, wholehearted response to the gospel. When you truly understand what God has done for you, obedience stops feeling like a burden and starts feeling like the only reasonable response.

Then Paul draws out the contrast. When you were slaves to sin, you were "free from the control of righteousness." In other words, sin gave you complete freedom from doing what was right. And what did that freedom produce? "Things you are now ashamed of." Sin's version of freedom is a dead end. It feels like liberty, but it leads to shame and death.

But now that you've been "set free from sin and have become slaves of God," the result is holiness, and the end is eternal life. Real freedom isn't the absence of all authority. It's being under the right authority, the one who made you, loves you, and knows what's best for you.

THE MOST FAMOUS VERSE IN THE CHAPTER

Paul finishes with a sentence so perfectly constructed that it has been memorized by millions: "For the wages of sin is death, but the gift of God is eternal life in Christ Jesus our Lord."

Two employers. Two payment methods. Two outcomes.

Sin pays wages. You earn death. It's what you deserve. It's the fair, calculated result of a life spent in rebellion against God. There's nothing surprising about it. You worked for it, and you got paid.

But God gives a gift. You don't earn eternal life. You can't. It's freely given, completely undeserved, and received only through being united to Christ Jesus. The word "gift" is doing all the heavy lifting in that sentence. Everything about the Christian life, from beginning to end, is a gift.

That single verse captures the entire argument of the first six chapters of Romans. The problem is sin. The penalty is death. The solution is grace. And the result is life.

WHAT THIS MEANS FOR US

First, grace is not permission to sin. This is the most important lesson of the chapter. Some people hear "you are saved by grace, not by works" and think that means behavior doesn't matter. Paul says the opposite. Grace changes you. It frees you from sin's control precisely so that you can live differently. If grace hasn't changed how you live, something has gone wrong in how you've understood it.

Second, your baptism means more than you think. It's easy to treat baptism as just a thing Christians do, a box to check. Paul says it's the moment you died and rose again. Every time you're tempted to go back to your old life, your baptism stands as a reminder: that person is dead. You don't live there anymore.

Third, remember who you are. The secret to fighting sin isn't willpower. It's identity. When you know who you are in Christ, dead to sin and alive to God, temptation loses its logic. You don't resist sin by gritting your teeth harder. You resist it by remembering that it has no claim on you.

Fourth, everyone serves something. The question isn't whether you'll be devoted to something but what you'll be devoted to. Sin is a brutal master that pays in death. God is a gracious master who gives the gift of life. The choice seems obvious when you put it that way, but sin has a way of making slavery look like freedom. Don't be fooled.

TALKING POINTS

1. **Paul says Christians have "died to sin."** If that's true, why do Christians still struggle with temptation? What's the

difference between sin having no legal claim on you and sin having no influence on you?

2. **Paul uses baptism as proof that Christians can't keep living in sin.** What does your baptism mean to you? If you haven't been baptized, what do you think Paul would say to you about it?

3. **Paul tells Christians to "count yourselves dead to sin but alive to God."** What would it look like practically, maybe in a situation at school or with friends, to remind yourself of who you are in Christ instead of giving in to temptation?

4. **Paul says everyone is a slave to something: either to sin or to God.** Do you agree? Can you think of examples where people think they're free but are actually controlled by something, whether that's popularity, money, approval, or something else?

5. **The chapter ends with "the wages of sin is death, but the gift of God is eternal life."** Why do you think Paul uses the word "wages" for sin but "gift" for eternal life? What does that difference reveal about how sin and God each operate?

The old self is dead. The new self is alive. But if the Christian life is supposed to be this clean break from sin, why does it still feel like a war inside? Why does doing the right thing feel so hard sometimes?

Paul knows that struggle. Better than you might think.

Turn the page.

6

THE WAR INSIDE

Robert Louis Stevenson's *The Strange Case of Dr. Jekyll and Mr. Hyde* tells the story of a respected London doctor who discovers a way to separate the two sides of his nature. Dr. Jekyll is educated, decent, and admired. But there's something else inside him, a darker self that craves the things Jekyll knows are wrong. So he creates a potion that lets that darker self loose. He calls this other version of himself Mr. Hyde.

At first, Jekyll thinks he's in control. He can drink the potion, become Hyde, do whatever he wants, and then switch back. Two lives. Two identities. No consequences. But it doesn't stay that way. Hyde starts showing up without the potion. The dark side gets stronger. Jekyll finds himself becoming the person he hates, doing the things he swore he would never do, and no amount of willpower can stop it. The man who wanted to control evil discovers that evil is controlling him.

That's Romans 7.

This is the chapter where Paul describes an experience so honest, so raw, that people have argued about it for two thousand years. It's about someone who knows what is right, loves what is right, and desperately wants to do what is right, but keeps failing. Over and over again. It's the most personal chapter in Romans, and also one of the most uncomfortable.

But before Paul gets to the struggle, he has to explain how it starts. And it starts with a question about the law.

FREE FROM THE LAW

At the end of Romans 6, Paul said that Christians are "not under the law but under grace." That's a bold statement. The law of Moses was the foundation of Jewish life for over a thousand years. It was God's own revelation, written on stone tablets, cherished by generations. So when Paul says Christians have been freed from it, he knows he's going to raise eyebrows.

To explain, he uses a comparison from marriage. Under Jewish law, a married woman is bound to her husband as long as he lives. If she leaves him and marries someone else while he's still alive, she's committed adultery. But if her husband dies, she's free. She can marry again without any guilt. Death ends the contract.

Paul's point isn't to give marriage advice. He's making an analogy. Christians were once bound to the law the way a wife is bound to her husband. But through the death of Christ, that binding relationship has been terminated. We "died to the law" through the body of Christ, so that we could belong to another: to Christ himself, risen from the dead.

This doesn't mean the law was bad. Paul will make that very clear. It means the law was never designed to be your savior. It was designed to reveal sin, not to remove it. Now that

Christ has come, believers serve God "in the new way of the Spirit, and not in the old way of the written code."

But this immediately creates another question. If the law brings sin to light but can't save you from it, does that make the law itself sinful?

IS THE LAW THE VILLAIN?

"What shall we say, then? Is the law sinful?"

Paul's answer is instant: "Certainly not!"

Then he begins one of the most intensely personal passages in all of his letters. He shifts into first person. "I." "Me." This isn't abstract theology anymore. Paul is telling his own story, or at least using himself to illustrate a universal human experience.

"I would not have known what sin was had it not been for the law. For I would not have known what coveting really was if the law had not said, 'You shall not covet.'"

This is a profound observation. Before someone tells you "don't touch that," you might never have thought about touching it. But the moment the rule appears, something inside you wakes up. A desire that was sleeping suddenly opens its eyes. The command not to covet didn't create the selfishness in Paul's heart, but it did expose it. Like turning on a light in a dark room, the law revealed what was already there.

Paul goes further. He says that sin, seizing the opportunity provided by the commandment, "produced in me every kind of coveting." Sin used the law like a foothold, a launching pad. The command said "don't," and something in him said, "now I want to."

Does that make the law evil? No. The law is good. It did exactly what it was supposed to do: it showed what sin really is. Paul compares it to realizing just how deadly a disease is. "In order that sin might be recognized as sin, it used what is good to bring about my death, so that through the commandment sin might become utterly sinful."

The law is like an X-ray machine. An X-ray shows you the broken bone, but it doesn't heal it. You don't blame the X-ray for the break. You're actually grateful it revealed the problem so you could get proper treatment. That's the law's role. It diagnoses. It doesn't cure.

THE STRUGGLE

Now Paul moves into the section that has gripped readers for centuries. He shifts to present tense, and the intensity goes up dramatically.

"I do not understand what I do. For what I want to do I do not do, but what I hate I do."

Read that again slowly. This is someone who is fully aware of the right thing. They want to do it. They intend to do it. But when the moment comes, they find themselves doing the exact opposite. And they hate it.

Paul continues: "If I do what I do not want to do, I agree that the law is good." In other words, the very fact that he hates his sin proves that his mind agrees with the law. He knows it's right. His conscience is intact. The problem isn't that he doesn't know what's good. The problem is that he can't seem to do it consistently.

"As it is, it is no longer I myself who do it, but it is sin living in me."

This is not Paul making excuses. He's not saying, "It wasn't really me; the devil made me do it." He's describing the experience of being pulled in two directions at once. Part of him, the renewed part, loves God's law and wants to obey it. But another part, what he calls "sin living in me," pulls him the other way. He feels like a battleground where two armies are fighting for control.

"For I know that good itself does not dwell in me, that is, in my sinful nature. For I have the desire to do what is good, but I cannot carry it out. For I do not do the good I want to do, but the evil I do not want to do, this I keep on doing."

This is some of the most relatable writing in the entire Bible. You don't have to be a first-century apostle to know this feeling. It's the student who decides tonight they won't look at their phone during homework and then picks it up five minutes later without even thinking about it. It's the kid who promises to stop gossiping about a classmate and catches the words coming out of their mouth before lunch. It's the person who kneels by their bed and prays for patience and loses their temper before breakfast.

Wanting to do right and doing right are not the same thing. And the gap between them is where the agony lives.

TWO LAWS AT WAR

Paul steps back and describes the situation in terms of competing forces. "So I find this law at work: although I want to do good, evil is right there with me. For in my inner being I delight in God's law; but I see another law at work in me, waging war against the law of my mind and making me a prisoner of the law of sin at work within me."

There are two "laws" operating inside this person. One is the law of the mind, which agrees with God and loves his commands. The other is the law of sin, which operates in the body and constantly pulls toward disobedience. These two forces are at war, and in this chapter, the war is being lost. The person who delights in God's law is being taken prisoner by sin.

This is not a picture of someone who doesn't care about God. It's a picture of someone who cares deeply about God but is trying to fight sin with the wrong weapon. They're relying on the law, on willpower, on moral knowledge, on knowing what's right. And those things are not enough. Knowing the right answer on the test doesn't mean you have the strength to live it.

The law can tell you what to do. It cannot give you the power to do it.

THE CRY

All of this builds to one of the most famous outcries in Scripture: "What a wretched man I am! Who will rescue me from this body that is subject to death?"

This is not a casual question. It's a scream. It's the cry of someone who has exhausted every resource, tried every strategy, and hit the bottom. They know they can't save themselves. They know the law can't save them. They know willpower can't save them. All that's left is to cry out for help.

And then, immediately, comes the answer: "Thanks be to God, who delivers me through Jesus Christ our Lord!"

The rescue doesn't come from trying harder. It doesn't come from more rules. It doesn't come from better self-discipline. It comes from a person. Jesus Christ. And it comes through what Jesus has done, not through what we manage to do.

Paul closes the chapter with a summary that captures the whole tension: "So then, I myself in my mind am a slave to God's law, but in my sinful nature a slave to the law of sin."

That's where things stand at the end of Romans 7. The struggle is real. The desire for God is genuine. But the power to follow through is missing. Something more is needed.

And that something is exactly what Paul unveils in the next chapter.

WHAT THIS MEANS FOR US

First, the law is good, but it was never meant to save you. God's commands are holy and right. They show us what God is like and what he expects. But knowing the rules doesn't give you the power to keep them. If you've ever felt frustrated that you know what you should do and still can't manage to do it, you're in good company. That frustration is actually evidence that your conscience is working properly.

Second, the inner struggle is real and normal. If you're a Christian and you still struggle with sin, that doesn't mean something is wrong with your faith. Romans 7 shows that the struggle between wanting to do right and being pulled toward wrong is a universal human experience. The fact that you hate your sin and wish you could stop is actually a sign that God is at work in you. People who are completely comfortable with their sin are in a much more dangerous place than people who are fighting it.

Third, willpower alone is not the answer. Paul was one of the most disciplined people who ever lived. If sheer determination could conquer sin, he would have done it. But he couldn't, and neither can you. The Christian life was never designed to run on willpower. It was designed to run on the Holy Spirit. The solution to the struggle in Romans 7 is not "try harder." It's "look to Romans 8."

Fourth, honesty about your struggles is a sign of maturity, not weakness. Paul doesn't pretend to have it all together. He admits the war. He names the failure. He screams for help. And then he thanks God for the rescue. That's the pattern for every Christian: honesty about the problem, trust in the Rescuer.

TALKING POINTS

1. **Paul says the law showed him what sin was but couldn't stop him from sinning.** Can you think of a rule in your own life (from parents, school, or church) that you knew was right but still had trouble obeying? What made it hard to follow, even when you agreed with it?

2. **Paul writes, "What I want to do I do not do, but what I hate I do."** Have you ever experienced this kind of inner conflict? What did it feel like to know the right thing and still do the wrong thing?

3. **Some people think that if you're a Christian, you shouldn't struggle with sin anymore.** How does Romans 7 challenge that idea? What's the difference between struggling with sin and being comfortable with it?

4. **Paul's cry in verse 24, "Who will rescue me?" is followed immediately by thanks to God through Jesus Christ.** Why do you think Paul moves so quickly from despair to gratitude? What does that tell us about where real help comes from?

5. **Romans 7 is full of the law but almost completely silent about the Holy Spirit.** Why do you think that matters? What might Paul be showing us about what happens when we try to fight sin without the Spirit's help?

The battle has been described. The cry for help has gone up. And the answer is about to arrive. Everything Paul has been building toward since the beginning of the letter reaches its climax in the next chapter, and it begins with the greatest sentence he ever wrote.

Turn the page.

7

NOTHING CAN SEPARATE US

At the end of *E.T. the Extra-Terrestrial*, everything seems lost. E.T. is dying. The government has swarmed Elliott's house. Scientists are poking and prodding, and there's nothing a ten-year-old boy can do to save his friend. Elliott holds E.T.'s hand and says goodbye.

And then, just when all hope is gone, E.T.'s heart begins to glow. He's alive. Somehow, against every expectation, life has defeated death. What follows is one of the most famous scenes in cinema history: Elliott and his friends racing through the streets on their bicycles, E.T. hidden in the basket, with government vehicles in pursuit. When it looks like they've been cornered, the bikes lift off the ground and soar across the sky, silhouetted against the full moon. No power on earth can keep them from reaching their destination.

That image, of being lifted above every obstacle, beyond the reach of every threat, carried by a power that nothing in this world can stop, captures the spirit of Romans 8.

This is the chapter that everything in Paul's letter has been building toward. Romans 1–3 showed us the problem:

everyone is guilty. Romans 3–5 gave us the solution: justification by grace through faith. Romans 6 explained that grace changes how we live. Romans 7 exposed the frustration of trying to fight sin with the law alone. And now Romans 8 gives us what we've been waiting for: the full, breathtaking picture of life in the Holy Spirit.

It starts with the greatest opening line Paul ever wrote. And it ends with the most triumphant paragraph in all of Scripture.

NO CONDEMNATION

"Therefore, there is now no condemnation for those who are in Christ Jesus."

After everything Paul has described, the guilt and the grace, the struggle and the cry for help, this sentence lands like sunrise after a long, dark night. No condemnation. Not "less condemnation." Not "condemnation if you mess up badly enough." None. Zero. The verdict has been pronounced, and it is permanent.

Why? Because "through Christ Jesus the law of the Spirit who gives life has set you free from the law of sin and death."

Romans 7 ended with a person trapped between two laws: the law of the mind that loves God and the law of sin that drags you down. Romans 8 introduces a new law, a more powerful one: the law of the Spirit of life. It doesn't just manage the conflict. It breaks the chains. The Spirit does what willpower and the written law could never do.

Paul explains how: "For what the law was powerless to do because it was weakened by the flesh, God did by sending his own Son in the likeness of sinful flesh to be a sin offering." The law couldn't save you, not because it was bad, but because your sinful nature made it impossible to keep. So God stepped in personally. He sent his Son. Jesus took on real human flesh, lived a real human life, and died as a real sacrifice for sin. God "condemned sin in the flesh" of his Son, so that you wouldn't be condemned yourself.

And the purpose of all this? "In order that the righteous requirement of the law might be fully met in us, who do not live according to the flesh but according to the Spirit."

The law's demands haven't been cancelled. They're being fulfilled, not by your straining effort, but by the Spirit's power working through you. What Romans 7 couldn't accomplish through human effort, Romans 8 accomplishes through divine power.

TWO WAYS TO LIVE

Paul then draws a sharp line between two ways of living: according to the flesh and according to the Spirit. "Those who live according to the flesh have their minds set on what the flesh desires; but those who live in accordance with the Spirit have their minds set on what the Spirit desires."

This is about direction, not perfection. It's about what you're oriented toward, what occupies your thinking, what shapes your decisions. The person living according to the flesh is fundamentally self-directed. The person living according to the Spirit is fundamentally God-directed.

Paul doesn't sugarcoat the stakes: "The mind governed by the flesh is death, but the mind governed by the Spirit is life and peace." And then, even more bluntly: "The mind governed by the flesh is hostile to God; it does not submit to God's law, nor can it do so."

This is why Romans 7's struggle was so agonizing. Without the Spirit, you can't keep God's law no matter how hard you try. Your fallen nature is actively hostile to God. It's not just weak. It's opposed. Only the Spirit can break that opposition and bring life and peace.

Then Paul drops a statement that defines who is and isn't a Christian: "If anyone does not have the Spirit of Christ, they do not belong to Christ." Being a Christian is more than church membership or moral behavior or doctrinal knowledge. It's about having the Spirit of God living inside you. That's the dividing line.

And if the Spirit is in you, Paul says, your body may still be subject to death because of sin, "but the Spirit gives life because of righteousness." Even more, the same Spirit who raised Jesus from the dead "will also give life to your mortal bodies." The Spirit isn't just helping you live better today. He's guaranteeing your resurrection tomorrow.

CHILDREN OF GOD

This leads Paul to one of the warmest passages in all his letters. "For those who are led by the Spirit of God are the children of God. The Spirit you received does not make you slaves, so that you live in fear again; rather, the Spirit you received brought about your adoption to sonship. And by him we cry, 'Abba, Father.'"

"Abba" is the Aramaic word for "Father," and it's intimate, personal, close. It's the word Jesus himself used when he prayed to God. Paul is saying that the same Spirit who connected Jesus to his Father now connects you to that same Father. You are not a slave cowering before a master. You are a child calling out to a dad.

"The Spirit himself testifies with our spirit that we are God's children." This is the inward assurance that every Christian receives: the quiet, steady confidence that you belong to God. Not because you earned it. Not because you're good enough. Because his Spirit lives in you and tells you so.

And if you're a child, Paul says, then you're also an heir. "Now if we are children, then we are heirs, heirs of God and co-heirs with Christ." Everything that belongs to Christ belongs to you. His resurrection. His glory. His inheritance. All of it. You don't just get saved. You get everything.

But Paul adds an honest clause: "if indeed we share in his sufferings in order that we may also share in his glory." The road to glory passes through suffering. It did for Jesus, and it will for his followers. But the suffering is not the end of the story. It's the road that leads to something unimaginably good.

GROANING AND HOPING

Paul now widens the lens from your personal experience to the entire created universe. And what he sees is a world in pain, but a world with hope.

"I consider that our present sufferings are not worth comparing with the glory that will be revealed in us."

That's a massive claim. Paul, who had been beaten, imprisoned, shipwrecked, and stoned, says that all of it doesn't even register on the scale when compared with what's coming.

The creation itself, Paul says, is "waiting in eager expectation for the children of God to be revealed." The natural world has been caught up in humanity's fall. It was "subjected to frustration" and is in "bondage to decay." Earthquakes, disease, death, the slow crumbling of everything: creation groans under the weight of a broken world. But it groans the way a woman groans in labor. The pain is real, but it's leading somewhere. Something is about to be born.

And Christians groan too. "We ourselves, who have the firstfruits of the Spirit, groan inwardly as we wait eagerly for our adoption to sonship, the redemption of our bodies." We have the Spirit now, which is like a down payment on the full inheritance. But we don't have everything yet. Our bodies still get sick. Our hearts still break. We live in the gap between "already saved" and "not yet fully restored."

What sustains us in that gap? Hope. "For in this hope we were saved."

And when we don't even know how to pray through the pain, the Spirit steps in: "The Spirit himself intercedes for us through wordless groans." Even our inability to pray is covered. The Spirit translates our inarticulate pain into prayers that align perfectly with God's will.

THE UNBREAKABLE CHAIN

Then Paul makes one of the most comforting statements in the Bible: "And we know that in all things God works for the good of those who love him, who have been called according to his purpose."

Not some things. All things. That doesn't mean everything

that happens is good. It means God is able to weave even the worst circumstances into a larger plan that ultimately serves your good and his glory. The word "works" implies active, ongoing involvement. God isn't watching from a distance. He's working in the middle of the mess.

Paul then traces a chain of divine actions that stretches from eternity past to eternity future: "For those God foreknew he also predestined to be conformed to the image of his Son. And those he predestined, he also called; those he called, he also justified; those he justified, he also glorified."

Foreknew. Predestined. Called. Justified. Glorified. Five links in a chain, and not one of them is broken. Notice that the last verb, "glorified," is in the past tense, even though it hasn't happened yet. Paul is so confident in God's plan that he speaks of the future as if it's already done. In God's mind, it is.

THE TRIUMPH

Now Paul pulls it all together in a crescendo that has echoed through every century since he wrote it.

"What, then, shall we say in response to these things? If God is for us, who can be against us?" Let that sink in. The God who planned your salvation before the world began, who sent his Son to die for you, who raised him from the dead, who gave you his Spirit, who adopted you into his family, who is working all things for your good, that God is for you. And if he is for you, no opposition in the universe matters.

"He who did not spare his own Son, but gave him up for us all, how will he not also, along with him, graciously give us all things?" The logic is airtight. If God gave you the most costly gift imaginable (his own Son), he will certainly not withhold anything else you need.

"Who will bring any charge against those whom God has chosen? It is God who justifies. Who then is the one who condemns? No one. Christ Jesus who died, more than that, who was raised to life, is at the right hand of God and is also interceding for us."

Every accuser is silenced. Satan, your own conscience, the memory of your worst failures: none of them can stick a charge on you that God hasn't already dealt with. Jesus died for those sins. Jesus was raised to prove the payment was accepted. And right now, at this very moment, Jesus is at God's right hand, speaking up on your behalf.

And then Paul asks the question that brings the whole chapter to its climax: "Who shall separate us from the love of Christ? Shall trouble or hardship or persecution or famine or nakedness or danger or sword?"

Paul lists the worst things that can happen to a human being. He's not being hypothetical. He experienced most of these personally. And his answer is absolute:

"No, in all these things we are more than conquerors through him who loved us." Not just survivors. Not just scrapers-by. More than conquerors. We don't merely endure. We triumph, because the one who loves us is stronger than anything that comes against us.

Then Paul delivers his final, glorious verdict: "For I am convinced that neither death nor life, neither angels nor demons, neither the present nor the future, nor any powers, neither height nor depth, nor anything else in all creation, will be able to separate us from the love of God that is in Christ Jesus our Lord."

He ransacks the universe for threats. Death? Can't do it. Life with all its complications? Can't do it. Supernatural powers? Can't do it. Time, whether present or future? Can't do it. The highest height or the deepest depth? Can't do it. Anything else you can imagine? Can't do it.

Nothing. Absolutely nothing. Can separate you from the love of God in Christ Jesus.

That's how Romans 8 ends. That's where Paul has been taking you since the very first verse of the letter. From guilt to grace, from condemnation to no condemnation, from the slavery of sin to the freedom of the Spirit, from groaning in the present to glory in the future, from fear to the unshakable, inexhaustible, irrevocable love of God.

WHAT THIS MEANS FOR US

First, the Christian life runs on the Spirit, not on willpower. Romans 7 showed what happens when you try to obey God in your own strength. Romans 8 shows what happens when the Spirit takes over. If your faith feels exhausting, the problem might not be that you're not trying hard enough. It might be that you're not relying on the Spirit enough.

Second, you are God's child, and nothing changes that. Adoption isn't temporary. God didn't bring you into his family on a trial basis. The Spirit himself confirms it. You belong. Even on your worst day, you are still his child, still loved, still held.

Third, suffering is not the end of the story. Paul doesn't pretend suffering isn't real. He calls it what it is. But he insists that it is temporary and that what's coming after it is so glorious it makes the pain look small. The groaning is real. The glory is bigger.

Fourth, God's love is the most secure thing in the universe. Not your commitment to God. His commitment to you. Paul doesn't say, "Nothing can cause you to stop loving God." He says nothing can separate you from God's love for you. The anchor of your salvation isn't your grip on God. It's his grip on you.

TALKING POINTS

1. **Paul opens the chapter by declaring "no condemnation" for those in Christ.** Why do you think so many Christians still feel condemned? What's the difference between conviction (the Spirit pointing out sin so you can deal with it) and condemnation (feeling rejected by God)?

2. **Paul says the Spirit gives us the right to cry "Abba, Father."** What does it mean to you that God invites you to address him in such a personal, intimate way? How does that change the way you think about prayer?

3. **Paul writes that "the whole creation has been groaning" and that even Christians "groan inwardly."** Why do you think groaning is such an important part of the Christian life right now? What are we groaning for?

4. **The chapter says God works "all things" for the good of those who love him.** Does that mean everything that happens to you is good? What's the difference between something being good and God working it for good?

5. **Paul ends with a list of things that cannot separate us from God's love.** If you could add one more thing to that list

from your own life, something you sometimes worry might cut you off from God, what would it be? How does Paul's answer speak to that fear?

The theology is in place. The Spirit has been given. God's love has been declared unbreakable. But Paul isn't finished. There's a question hanging over everything he's said, a question about the people who received God's promises first. What about Israel?

Turn the page.

8

HAS GOD GIVEN UP ON ISRAEL?

In the movie *Remember the Titans*, a high school football team in Virginia is forced to integrate in the early 1970s. Black players and white players who have grown up in separate worlds are thrown together on the same squad, under the same coaches, wearing the same jersey. It's uncomfortable. It's tense. Some players want nothing to do with each other.

But Coach Boone has a plan. He doesn't just want a team that looks integrated on paper. He wants a team that actually plays as one. The whole movie is the story of how that happens, how two groups who were divided learn to trust each other, fight for each other, and eventually become something neither could have been alone.

There's a moment when the team's unity is threatened from the outside. People in the community don't want integration to work. They try to sabotage it. And you find yourself asking: Is this thing going to fall apart? Was the coach's vision ever going to hold?

Romans 9–11 asks a similar question, but on a much bigger scale. Paul has just finished explaining the gospel of grace, available to everyone who believes, Jew and Gentile alike. But this raises a massive question that no honest Jewish reader could avoid: what about Israel? God chose them. He made promises to them. He gave them the law, the temple, the prophets, the covenants. For two thousand years they were at the center of his plan. And now most of them have rejected their own Messiah.

So has God's plan failed? Has he abandoned his people? Has his word come to nothing?

Paul's answer takes three chapters, and it's one of the most complex arguments in the entire Bible. But at its core, it's about one thing: the faithfulness of God.

THE ACHE IN PAUL'S HEART

Paul doesn't begin with theology. He begins with tears. "I have great sorrow and unceasing anguish in my heart. For I could wish that I myself were cursed and cut off from Christ for the sake of my people, those of my own race, the people of Israel."

Stop and feel the weight of that. Paul, the man who just finished writing "nothing can separate us from the love of God," says he would trade his own salvation, his own eternity, if it could save his fellow Jews. He knows it can't. Only Christ can do that. But the fact that he would even think it tells you how deeply he cares.

Then he lists what makes Israel's rejection so painful. These are the people who received the adoption as God's special nation. They were given the glory of God's visible presence. They received the covenants, the law, the temple worship, the promises. The great patriarchs, Abraham, Isaac, and Jacob, belong to them. And from their family line came the Messiah himself, "who is God over all, forever praised."

No nation in history was given more. And yet most of them said no to the very Savior their entire existence had been pointing toward.

So here's the question that hangs over everything: has God's word failed?

TWO ISRAELS

Paul's answer begins with a statement that changes the entire conversation: "It is not as though God's word had failed. For not all who are descended from Israel are Israel."

There it is. The key to the whole section. There are two Israels.

One is ethnic Israel, the physical nation, every person born into the Jewish people. The other is spiritual Israel, the believing remnant within the nation, those who share not just Abraham's bloodline but Abraham's faith.

God's promises to ethnic Israel were about service, not salvation. He chose the Jewish nation to play a specific, glorious role in his plan of redemption. They would receive the law. They would preserve the Scriptures. They would carry the line of the Messiah through history until the right moment came. And they did. Every single one of those purposes was accomplished. God's word did not fail.

But being chosen to serve God's plan is not the same as being chosen for personal salvation. Serving in God's plan didn't automatically mean every individual Jew was saved. Salvation has always been, for everyone, a matter of personal faith.

Paul proves this with examples from Israel's own history. God chose Isaac, not Ishmael, even though both were sons of Abraham. God chose Jacob, not Esau, even though they were twins, born to the same parents. And God made these choices before the boys were born, "before they had done anything good or bad."

The point isn't that God was picking who would go to heaven and who would go to hell. The point is that God has always had the right to choose who would serve in his plan and how. He selected Isaac and Jacob to be the founders of the nation through which the Messiah would come. Whether those individuals were personally saved was a separate matter entirely.

IS GOD UNFAIR?

Paul knows this raises a question: "Is God unjust?"

His answer: "Not at all!"

God has the sovereign right to use anyone he chooses for his purposes, whether that person is a believer or not. To illustrate, Paul points to Pharaoh. God told Pharaoh, "I raised you up for this very purpose, that I might display my power in you and that my name might be proclaimed in all the earth." Pharaoh was not a believer. He was a brutal tyrant. But God used him anyway, as part of the story that led to Israel's liberation from Egypt. Being used by God didn't save Pharaoh. It served God's larger purpose.

Paul then uses the image of a potter and clay. A potter has the right to make different kinds of vessels from the same lump. Some are for special use, some for ordinary use. The clay doesn't get to complain about the potter's decisions. In the same way, God has the right to shape his plan the way he sees fit. He can use an entire nation for his purposes without being obligated to save every individual within it.

This isn't cruelty. It's sovereignty. God made the plan, God formed the nation, and God has the right to distinguish between those he uses for service and those who respond to him in faith for salvation.

And who are those who respond in faith? Paul calls them "vessels of mercy," and he says God prepared them in advance for glory. These are the remnant, the believers. And they don't come only from Israel. They come "also from the Gentiles." Paul backs this up with Old Testament prophecies from Hosea and Isaiah: God promised to call "not my people" his people, and to save a remnant of Israel even when the nation as a whole went astray.

WHY ISRAEL STUMBLED

In Romans 9:30–10:21, Paul shifts from the question of God's rights to the question of Israel's responsibility. And here the issue becomes crystal clear.

"What then shall we say? That the Gentiles, who did not pursue righteousness, have obtained it, a righteousness that is by faith; but the people of Israel, who pursued the law as the way of righteousness, have not attained their goal."

The Gentiles weren't even looking for God's righteousness, and they found it, because they received it by faith. The Jews were looking for it intensely, but they were looking in the wrong place. They were trying to earn it through obedience to the law instead of receiving it as a gift through faith.

Paul puts it bluntly: "Since they did not know the righteousness of God and sought to establish their own, they did not submit to God's righteousness." Israel's problem wasn't ignorance in the sense that they had never heard. Their problem was that they rejected God's way of salvation and insisted on their own. They wanted to be right with God on the basis of what they did rather than on the basis of what God did for them through Christ.

"Christ is the culmination of the law so that there may be righteousness for everyone who believes." Everything the law pointed to has arrived in Jesus. He is the goal the law was always driving toward. And now righteousness is available to everyone, Jew or Gentile, who believes.

Paul then makes it clear that salvation is not complicated. "If you declare with your mouth, 'Jesus is Lord,' and believe in your heart that God raised him from the dead, you will be saved." It's the same for everyone. No ethnic prerequisites. No ritual requirements. "For there is no difference between Jew and Gentile. The same Lord is Lord of all and richly blesses all who call on him."

But then Paul asks a chain of questions that should haunt every reader: "How can they call on the one they have not believed in? And how can they believe in the one of whom they have not heard? And how can they hear without someone preaching to them?"

The gospel has to be shared. Faith comes from hearing the message. And the message has been shared. Israel heard it. Moses predicted it. Isaiah foretold it. The problem was not a lack of information. It was a refusal to believe.

NOT ABANDONED

In chapter 11, Paul asks the question one final time: "Did God reject his people?"

"By no means!"

Paul offers himself as proof. He is an Israelite, from the tribe of Benjamin, and he is saved. God has not thrown away every Jew. There has always been a remnant, a group of believers within the larger nation. In Elijah's day, when it seemed like all of Israel had turned to idol worship, God told Elijah that he had preserved seven thousand people who had not bowed to Baal. The same principle is at work now. "So too, at the present time there is a remnant chosen by grace."

Then Paul introduces one of his most vivid images. He compares God's people to an olive tree. The roots of the tree are the patriarchs, Abraham, Isaac, and Jacob. The natural branches are the Jewish people. Some of those branches were broken off because of unbelief. And wild branches, the Gentiles, were grafted in to share in the richness of the tree.

Paul warns the Gentile believers not to become arrogant about this. "You do not support the root, but the root supports you." The Gentiles didn't replace Israel. They were brought into a story that started with Israel. And if God didn't spare the natural branches when they turned away in unbelief, he won't spare the grafted-in branches either if they do the same.

But here's the hopeful part: the broken-off branches can be grafted back in. "If they do not persist in unbelief, they will be grafted in, for God is able to graft them in again." The door is not closed. Any Jewish person who turns to Christ in faith will be welcomed back into the people of God.

Paul then reveals what he calls a "mystery": "Israel has experienced a hardening in part until the full number of the Gentiles has come in. And in this way all Israel will be saved."

That phrase "all Israel" has been debated for centuries. Some think it means every Jewish person alive at some future moment will be converted. But in the context of everything Paul has been arguing, "all Israel" most likely refers to the full number of God's true people, the complete remnant drawn from both Jews and Gentiles throughout history, saved the same way anyone has ever been saved: by grace, through faith. There is no secret backup plan for Israel that bypasses Jesus. The way of salvation for Jews is the same as for everyone else. It always has been.

Paul wraps up this section with a breathtaking statement about God's dealings with both Jews and Gentiles: "For God has bound everyone over to disobedience so that he may have mercy on them all." No group gets to boast. Everyone was disobedient. Everyone needs mercy. And mercy is available to all.

THE OVERFLOW OF PRAISE

After three chapters of the most complex argument in the letter, Paul doesn't end with a conclusion. He ends with worship.

"Oh, the depth of the riches of the wisdom and knowledge of God! How unsearchable his judgments, and his paths beyond tracing out! Who has known the mind of the Lord? Or who has been his counselor? Who has ever given to God, that God should repay them? For from him and through him and to him are all things. To him be the glory forever! Amen."

When you've spent three chapters trying to trace the ways of God through the tangled history of Israel and the nations, the only fitting response is awe. God's plan is bigger than we can fully comprehend. His faithfulness runs deeper than we can measure. And his mercy reaches farther than anyone deserves.

WHAT THIS MEANS FOR US

First, God keeps his promises. That's the whole point of these chapters. If God failed Israel, how could we trust him with our own futures? But he didn't fail them. Every promise he made to the nation was fulfilled. And every promise he makes to you in Christ will be fulfilled too.

Second, being religious doesn't automatically mean being saved. Israel had more religious heritage than any people on earth, and most of them missed the Messiah standing right in front of them. Church attendance, Bible knowledge, and family tradition are wonderful things, but they don't substitute for personal faith in Jesus.

Third, God's plan is bigger than any one group. The gospel was never meant for one ethnicity or one culture. It has always been heading toward "everyone who believes." If you're tempted to think your group has a special claim on God, these chapters are a warning.

Fourth, the door is always open. No one is so far gone that they can't come back. If broken-off branches can be grafted in again, then no person and no group is beyond the reach of God's mercy. But the way back is always the same: faith in Christ.

TALKING POINTS

1. **Paul says there are two "Israels," one defined by ethnicity and one defined by faith.** Why do you think this

distinction was so hard for Jewish people to accept? Can you think of ways that people today confuse belonging to a group with having a personal relationship with God?

2. **Paul says Israel stumbled because they tried to earn righteousness through the law instead of receiving it by faith.** Why do you think people are so drawn to the idea of earning God's approval? What makes receiving a gift harder than working for a reward?

3. **The olive tree image shows Gentile believers grafted into a Jewish story.** Why does Paul warn the Gentile branches not to be arrogant? What happens when Christians forget that they were brought into a story that didn't start with them?

4. **Paul says that God "bound everyone over to disobedience so that he may have mercy on them all."** What does this tell us about how God views Jews and Gentiles? How does this statement level the playing field?

5. **After three difficult chapters, Paul breaks into a hymn of praise about the depth of God's wisdom.** Why do you think wrestling with hard questions about God sometimes leads to worship instead of more questions?

The theology is finished. The questions about Israel are answered. God's faithfulness stands. But if all of this is true, if we really have been justified, freed, adopted, and secured by an unbreakable love, then what does the rest of our lives look like?

Paul is about to tell us.

Turn the page.

9

WHAT THE GOSPEL LOOKS LIKE ON MONDAY MORNING

Have you ever watched someone do something so kind, so generous, so completely selfless that it made you want to be a better person? Maybe a coach stayed late every day to help a struggling player. Maybe a friend gave up something they wanted so someone else could have it. Maybe you saw a stranger help somebody when they thought no one was watching and nobody would ever reward.

Something happens inside you when you see that. You don't just admire it. You feel pulled toward it. You think, "I want to live like that."

That's what Romans 12–13 are designed to do. For eleven chapters, Paul has been explaining what God has done for us. He has proven that we're all guilty. He has revealed that God justifies the guilty freely by his grace. He has shown that the Spirit gives us power to live a new life. He has declared that absolutely nothing can separate us from God's love. And he has defended God's faithfulness through the complicated history of Israel.

Now he asks: so what are you going to do about it?

This is where the gospel hits the ground. This is where theology turns into Tuesday. Paul is done explaining what God has done. Now he's going to describe what a life shaped by grace actually looks like, in your family, your friendships, your church, your neighborhood, and even your relationship with the government.

And it all starts with an altar.

THE LIVING SACRIFICE

"Therefore, I urge you, brothers and sisters, in view of God's mercy, to offer your bodies as a living sacrifice, holy and pleasing to God. This is your true and proper worship."

That word "therefore" is doing more work than almost any word in the letter. It reaches all the way back to Romans 1 and gathers up everything Paul has said: the guilt, the grace, the justification, the freedom, the Spirit, the unbreakable love. All of that is the "mercy" Paul is talking about. And in view of all that mercy, here is the only reasonable response: give God everything.

In the Old Testament, worshipers brought animals to the altar as sacrifices. The animal was killed and offered to God. Paul takes that image and flips it. You are the sacrifice. But you're not dead. You're alive. Your whole body, your hands, your feet, your mouth, your mind, belongs to God. Not just on Sunday mornings. Every day.

This is what real worship looks like. It's not limited to singing songs in a building. It's how you treat people at lunch. It's what you do with your phone when no one is watching. It's the way you talk about someone who isn't in the room. Every part of your life becomes an act of worship when it's offered to God.

Then Paul adds the second half of the equation: "Do not conform to the pattern of this world, but be transformed by the renewing of your mind. Then you will be able to test and approve what God's will is, his good, pleasing and perfect will."

Two forces are pulling on you every day. The world wants to squeeze you into its mold, to make you think the way everyone else thinks, value what everyone else values, chase what everyone else chases. But God wants to transform you from the inside out, starting with your mind. When the way you think changes, the way you live changes. And when the way you live changes, you start to see God's will clearly: what is good, what pleases him, what leads to the life you were designed for.

KNOW WHO YOU ARE

Paul's first practical instruction after the big appeal might surprise you. Before he tells you how to treat other people, he tells you how to think about yourself.

"Do not think of yourself more highly than you ought, but rather think of yourself with sober judgment, in accordance with the faith God has distributed to each of you."

The gospel destroys both arrogance and self-hatred. You can't be arrogant because everything you have is a gift. You can't hate yourself because God loved you enough to die for you. What's left is a clear-eyed, honest understanding of who you are: someone gifted by God, placed in a community, and called to serve.

Paul then uses the image of a human body. Just as a body has many parts, each with a different function, so the church is one body with many members. Some are gifted to prophesy.

Some are gifted to serve. Some are gifted to teach, to encourage, to give, to lead, to show mercy. No gift is unimportant. No member is unnecessary. The eye can't say to the hand, "I don't need you." The body works only when every part does its job.

This means two things for you. First, figure out what your gift is and use it. Don't sit on the sidelines wishing you had someone else's abilities. Use what God gave you. Second, stop comparing. The person who quietly serves behind the scenes is just as vital to the body as the person who teaches up front.

THE RECIPE FOR LOVE

Starting in verse 9, Paul launches into one of the most concentrated bursts of practical instruction in the entire Bible. Nearly every sentence is its own command, and together they form a recipe for what love looks like when it's real.

"Love must be sincere." That's the foundation. No faking it. No putting on a nice face while your heart is somewhere else. Genuine love, the kind God showed you, is the starting point for everything.

Then the ingredients come rapid-fire: "Hate what is evil; cling to what is good. Be devoted to one another in love. Honor one another above yourselves. Never be lacking in zeal, but keep your spiritual fervor, serving the Lord. Be joyful in hope, patient in affliction, faithful in prayer. Share with the Lord's people who are in need. Practice hospitality."

Read that list again slowly. Each phrase is a complete instruction for life. Be devoted. Honor others above yourself. Keep your passion burning. Stay joyful. Stay patient. Stay prayerful. Share what you have. Open your home.

This isn't a checklist you finish once. It's a description of the kind of person grace is making you into. Every line points back to the mercy of God in Romans 1–11. You can be devoted because God was devoted to you. You can be patient because God was patient with you. You can share because God gave everything to you.

WHEN PEOPLE HURT YOU

Then Paul addresses something every person faces: enemies. People who hurt you. People who wrong you.

"Bless those who persecute you; bless and do not curse."

That's hard enough. But Paul goes further.

"Do not repay anyone evil for evil. Be careful to do what is right in the eyes of everyone. If it is possible, as far as it depends on you, live at peace with everyone."

And then the sentence that cuts deepest: "Do not take revenge, my dear friends, but leave room for God's wrath, for it is written: 'It is mine to avenge; I will repay,' says the Lord."

When someone wrongs you, every instinct in your body screams for payback. Paul says: don't. Not because the wrong doesn't matter, but because justice belongs to God, not to you. He will handle it. Your job is different.

"If your enemy is hungry, feed him; if he is thirsty, give him something to drink."

This is not weakness. This is the most powerful thing a human being can do. When you respond to hatred with kindness, you break the cycle. You refuse to let evil set the terms. Paul puts it in a sentence that should be written on every wall: "Do not be overcome by evil, but overcome evil with good."

Evil wins when it makes you act like it. Good wins when you refuse.

RESPECT THE AUTHORITIES

Romans 13 opens with a topic that surprises some readers: the government. "Let everyone be subject to the governing authorities, for there is no authority except that which God has established."

Paul isn't saying every government is good. He knew better than most how corrupt governments could be. He had been beaten, jailed, and chased out of cities by authorities acting unjustly. But he's making a broader point: the concept of government, of ordered society with laws and courts and public servants, is part of God's design for the world.

The state's job is to restrain evil and promote good. "For rulers hold no terror for those who do right, but for those who do wrong." When the system works as God intended, the government punishes wrongdoing and protects the innocent. It is, Paul says, "God's servant for your good."

This is also why Christians pay taxes. The infrastructure of society, roads, courts, emergency services, defense, costs money. Paul says to give what you owe: "If you owe taxes, pay taxes; if revenue, then revenue; if respect, then respect; if honor, then honor."

Notice the last two items. Respect and honor. Even when you disagree with the people in power, you can disagree respectfully. The gospel doesn't make you a rebel against every authority. It makes you the kind of citizen who serves the common good because you serve a higher King.

LOVE IS THE WHOLE LAW

Paul then circles back to the theme that runs through everything: love. "Let no debt remain outstanding, except the continuing debt to love one another, for whoever loves others has fulfilled the law."

Think about that. All the commandments Paul could have listed, all the rules, all the requirements, and he says they all come down to one thing: "Love your neighbor as yourself." The commands against adultery, murder, stealing, coveting, and every other command, are all just specific applications of love. When you genuinely love someone, you won't harm them. Love doesn't wrong a neighbor. "Therefore love is the fulfillment of the law."

This doesn't mean the law doesn't matter. It means love is what the law was always driving at. When your heart is full of genuine love for the people around you, you naturally do what the law commands. Not from fear of punishment, but from the overflow of a heart that has been transformed by grace.

WAKE UP

Paul closes this section with an urgent reminder about the time. "And do this, understanding the present time: The hour has already come for you to wake up from your slumber, because our salvation is nearer now than when we first believed. The night is nearly over; the day is almost here."

Paul is talking about the return of Christ. Every day that passes brings us one day closer to the moment when Jesus comes back and sets everything right. The "night" is this present age, with all its darkness and struggle. The "day" is the age to come, when God's kingdom will be fully established.

And since that day is coming, Paul says, live like it. "Let us put aside the deeds of darkness and put on the armor of light. Let us behave decently, as in the daytime." When you know the sun is about to rise, you don't go back to bed. You get up and get ready.

The chapter ends with one of the most memorable commands in Paul's letters: "Clothe yourselves with the Lord Jesus Christ, and do not think about how to gratify the desires of the flesh."

Your clothing is your identity. What people see when they look at you. Paul says: put on Jesus. Let his character be what's visible in your life. Let his love, his patience, his courage, his humility be the first thing people notice. And stop spending your mental energy figuring out how to feed your selfishness. You have better things to do. The day is coming.

WHAT THIS MEANS FOR US

First, worship is a whole-life thing. It's not just what happens on Sunday. It's what happens when you offer your body, your decisions, your daily routine to God as an act of worship. The way you live is your loudest form of praise.

Second, love is the test of everything. If you're not sure whether something is right or wrong, ask whether it's loving. Love doesn't harm. Love serves. Love overcomes evil with good. Every command in the Bible is an expression of love, and love is the fulfillment of every command.

Third, how you respond to enemies reveals what you really believe. Anyone can be kind to the people who are kind to them. The gospel calls you to something harder and more powerful: blessing the people who hurt you, feeding the people who oppose you, and refusing to let their evil turn you into something you're not.

Fourth, the clock is ticking. Every day brings the return of Christ one day closer. That's not meant to scare you. It's meant to wake you up. Live with urgency. Live with purpose. Put on Jesus, and get to work.

TALKING POINTS

1. **Paul says to offer your body as a "living sacrifice."** What does that look like practically for someone your age? What areas of your life are hardest to hand over to God?

2. **Paul says "do not conform to the pattern of this world, but be transformed by the renewing of your mind."** What are some "patterns of this world" that you see pressuring people your age? How does a renewed mind help you resist that pressure?

3. **Paul tells us to "overcome evil with good."** Can you think of a specific situation where someone responded to cruelty with kindness, and it actually changed the outcome? Why is this so much harder than it sounds?

4. **Paul says love "fulfills the law."** Does that mean the specific commandments don't matter anymore, as long as you're being loving? Or does love make the commandments even more important? Explain your thinking.

5. **Paul ends by saying to "clothe yourselves with the Lord Jesus Christ."** If someone looked at your life this week, what would they say you were "wearing"? What would need to change for people to see more of Jesus in you?

The gospel changes how you worship, how you think, how you love, how you fight, and how you live. But there's still one more issue Paul needs to address: what happens when Christians disagree with each other?

Turn the page.

10

LIVING TOGETHER IN GRACE

In *The Karate Kid*, Daniel LaRusso moves to a new town and immediately runs into trouble. He doesn't fit in. He doesn't know the culture. And a group of karate students from the Cobra Kai dojo start making his life miserable. But then he meets Mr. Miyagi, the quiet maintenance man at his apartment complex, and everything starts to change.

Here's what makes the movie so good. It's not just a story about learning to fight. It's a story about learning to live. Mr. Miyagi doesn't just teach Daniel how to throw punches. He teaches him patience, respect, humility, and the difference between strength used to bully people and strength used to protect them. The climax isn't really the tournament. It's the moment Daniel finally understands that true strength isn't about dominating the people around you. It's about serving them.

That's the idea at the heart of Romans 14–16. Paul has spent the whole letter building an argument about grace. We are saved by grace, not by works. We are free from the law. We belong to Christ. We are filled with the Spirit. But now he faces a very practical question: what happens when people who share the same grace disagree with each other?

The church in Rome was made up of Jewish Christians and Gentile Christians, people from wildly different backgrounds, with different habits, different traditions, and different convictions about what was and wasn't acceptable behavior. And those differences were causing friction.

Paul's answer isn't "figure out who's right and make everyone else fall in line." His answer is far more demanding than that. It's "use your freedom to serve one another."

THE WEAK AND THE STRONG

Paul divides the Roman Christians into two groups. He calls them "the weak" and "the strong." These labels aren't about character or willpower. They're about the freedom of a person's conscience.

The "weak" were mostly Jewish Christians who still felt bound by Old Testament dietary laws and the observance of certain holy days. They ate only vegetables to make sure they never accidentally consumed meat that wasn't properly prepared according to Jewish standards. They treated certain days as sacred and set them apart from others. Their consciences wouldn't let them do otherwise.

The "strong" were mostly Gentile believers (along with some Jewish Christians like Paul himself) who understood that in Christ all foods are clean and no day is more sacred than another. They had a freedom of conscience that the weak didn't yet share.

Paul makes it clear that he personally agrees with the strong. He writes, "I am convinced, being fully persuaded in the Lord Jesus, that nothing is unclean in itself." Theologically, the strong are correct. But being correct doesn't give you the right to run over someone else's conscience. And this is where Paul's instructions get interesting.

ACCEPT, DON'T ARGUE

The first command is simple and sweeping: "Accept the one whose faith is weak, without quarreling over disputable matters."

Notice two things. First, Paul says to accept the weak, not to fix them. The word "accept" means more than tolerating someone's existence. It means welcoming them warmly into the fellowship, treating them as a genuine brother or sister, not as a project to be corrected. Second, Paul calls these issues "disputable matters." They're not core gospel truths. They're secondary questions on which sincere Christians can disagree. Matters of diet and days fall into this category. Matters of salvation and the lordship of Christ do not.

Then Paul lays down two prohibitions. The strong must not look down on the weak, and the weak must not condemn the strong. The temptation for the strong is contempt: "How can you be so immature?" The temptation for the weak is judgment: "How can you be so careless?" Both are forbidden, and for the same reason: "for God has accepted him."

That's the trump card. If God has welcomed this person into his family, who are you to show them the door? Paul puts it even more pointedly: "Who are you to judge someone else's servant? To their own master, servants stand or fall. And they will stand, for the Lord is able to make them stand."

Every believer answers to Christ, not to you. Your fellow Christian's conscience is between them and their Lord. You may think their scruples are unnecessary, or you may think their freedoms are reckless. Either way, they don't report to you.

DON'T DESTROY WHAT CHRIST DIED FOR

Paul then raises the stakes considerably. He shifts from how we regard each other to how we treat each other.

"If your brother or sister is distressed because of what you eat, you are no longer acting in love. Do not by your eating destroy someone for whom Christ died."

Think about what Paul is asking the strong to consider. Christ loved this person so much that he died for them. Are you really going to wound their conscience over a plate of food? Is your right to eat whatever you want more important than your brother's spiritual wellbeing?

Paul doesn't mince words: "Do not destroy the work of God for the sake of food." He's asking the strong to get their priorities straight. The kingdom of God is not about eating and drinking. It's about "righteousness, peace and joy in the Holy Spirit." Those are the things that matter. Food is trivial by comparison. Anyone who serves Christ by pursuing righteousness, peace, and joy "is pleasing to God and receives human approval."

So the strong should voluntarily limit their freedom. "It is better not to eat meat or drink wine or to do anything else that will cause your brother or sister to fall." This isn't weakness. It's love in action. It's the strong choosing to carry the weak rather than crush them.

Paul summarizes the principle beautifully: "Let us therefore make every effort to do what leads to peace and to mutual edification." The goal isn't winning the argument. The goal is building each other up.

FOLLOW CHRIST'S EXAMPLE

At the beginning of chapter 15, Paul gives the ultimate reason for all of this: "We who are strong ought to bear with the failings of the weak and not to please ourselves. Each of us should please our neighbors for their good, to build them up."

And then he points to the one person who modeled this perfectly: "For even Christ did not please himself."

If anyone had the right to please himself, it was Jesus. He was God in the flesh. He had every right, every authority, every justification for doing exactly what he wanted. But instead, he emptied himself. He served. He bore insults. He went to the cross. Not for his own benefit, but for ours.

If Christ, with all his power and all his rights, chose not to please himself, how can we, his followers, insist on pleasing ourselves at the expense of a weaker brother or sister?

Paul then prays for the Roman church: "May the God who gives endurance and encouragement give you the same attitude of mind toward each other that Christ Jesus had, so that with one mind and one voice you may glorify the God and Father of our Lord Jesus Christ."

That's the goal. Not uniformity on every issue. Unity in Christ. Not agreement on every detail of diet and practice. One mind and one voice in worship.

And then comes the command that wraps up the whole discussion: “Accept one another, then, just as Christ accepted you, in order to bring praise to God.”

The way you treat other Christians is an act of worship. When you welcome the person who disagrees with you on secondary matters, when you lay down your rights for the sake of someone else’s conscience, when you value the relationship over the argument, you bring praise to God. That’s the whole point.

JEWS AND GENTILES, TOGETHER

Paul then lifts his eyes to the bigger picture. The whole letter has been about how God’s grace reaches both Jews and Gentiles. Now he shows that this isn’t some afterthought. It was always the plan.

“For I tell you that Christ has become a servant of the Jews on behalf of God’s truth, so that the promises made to the patriarchs might be confirmed and, moreover, that the Gentiles might glorify God for his mercy.”

Then Paul strings together four Old Testament quotations from the Law, the Psalms, and the Prophets, all showing that God always intended for the Gentiles to praise him alongside Israel. The inclusion of the nations was not a plan B. It was built into the story from the beginning.

Paul closes this section with a benediction that overflows with hope: “May the God of hope fill you with all joy and peace as you trust in him, so that you may overflow with hope by the power of the Holy Spirit.”

Joy. Peace. Hope. Overflowing. By the power of the Holy Spirit. That’s what life together in grace is supposed to look like.

PAUL'S PLANS AND FRIENDS

The rest of Romans 15 and all of chapter 16 are deeply personal. Paul explains his travel plans. He wants to visit Rome on his way to Spain, where he hopes to break new ground for the gospel. But first he has to go to Jerusalem to deliver a financial gift that the Gentile churches have collected for the poor Jewish believers there. He asks the Roman Christians to pray for his safety and for the gift to be well received.

Then in chapter 16, Paul does something remarkable. He greets nearly thirty people by name. He mentions Phoebe, a servant of the church in Cenchreae, who likely carried the letter to Rome. He greets Priscilla and Aquila, his fellow workers who risked their lives for him. He mentions Andronicus and Junia, who were in Christ before he was. He names people from every walk of life, men and women, Jews and Gentiles, slaves and free.

This matters more than you might think. Romans isn't just a theological document. It was written to real people, people Paul knew and loved. The gospel isn't just an idea floating in the sky. It lands in real communities, in real houses, among real friends who eat together, pray together, disagree with each other, and choose grace over grievance.

Paul also includes a warning: "Watch out for those who cause divisions and put obstacles in your way that are contrary to the teaching you have learned. Keep away from them." Unity matters, but not at the expense of truth. There is a difference between secondary issues (where disagreement is permitted) and core gospel teaching (where it is not). Paul has been gracious about the former throughout chapters 14–15. He is firm about the latter here.

THE FINAL WORD

The letter ends the way it began: with the gospel.

"Now to him who is able to establish you in accordance with my gospel, the message I proclaim about Jesus Christ, in keeping with the revelation of the mystery hidden for long ages past, but now revealed and made known through the prophetic writings by the command of the eternal God, so that all the Gentiles might come to the obedience that comes from faith, to the only wise God be glory forever through Jesus Christ! Amen."

Everything circles back. The gospel Paul proclaimed in chapter 1 is the same gospel he celebrates in chapter 16. It was hidden in the Old Testament and revealed in Christ. It calls all nations to the obedience that comes from faith. And it brings glory to the only wise God, forever, through Jesus Christ.

Amen. That's how Romans ends. Not with a whimper, but with worship.

WHAT THIS MEANS FOR US

First, being right doesn't give you the right to be unkind. You may have a more educated conscience than someone else. You may understand grace better than someone else. But if your knowledge makes you arrogant instead of patient, you've missed the point. Strength in the Christian life is measured not by how much freedom you claim but by how much freedom you give up for the sake of others.

Second, unity doesn't require uniformity. Christians will disagree about secondary issues for as long as the church exists. The test of maturity is not whether you can force everyone to agree with you, but whether you can love someone you disagree with. The Roman church had to learn this. So does every church today.

Third, Christ is the model for everything. When you don't know how to handle a disagreement, look at Jesus. He didn't please himself. He served. He bore the burdens of others. He welcomed people who didn't deserve it. If you want to know what grace looks like in action, look at the cross.

Fourth, the gospel is for the whole world. Romans began with Paul declaring that the gospel is "the power of God that brings salvation to everyone who believes, first to the Jew, then to the Gentile." It ends with the same vision: all nations, every people, coming to faith and giving glory to God. That vision hasn't changed. And it includes you.

TALKING POINTS

1. **Paul says the strong should limit their freedom for the sake of the weak.** Can you think of a situation where giving up something you have the right to do would be the loving thing to do? What makes that kind of sacrifice hard?

2. **Paul says the kingdom of God is not about eating and drinking but about "righteousness, peace and joy in the Holy Spirit."** Why do you think Christians sometimes get more passionate about secondary issues than about these core realities? How can we keep the main thing the main thing?

3. **Paul says to "accept one another, just as Christ accepted you." Think about how Christ accepted you: while you were still a sinner, with nothing to offer.** How should that shape the way you treat other Christians, especially the ones who annoy you or see things differently?

4. **In Romans 16, Paul greets nearly thirty people by name, men and women, Jews and Gentiles, from all walks of life.** What does this tell you about what the early church actually looked like? How does it challenge or encourage the way you think about your own church community?

5. **Romans begins and ends with the gospel.** If you had to summarize the message of Romans in one sentence, based on everything you've read, what would that sentence be?

The book is finished.

But the story isn't. Romans wasn't written to be admired from a distance. It was written to change how you live. The God who justified the guilty, freed the enslaved, adopted the orphaned, and promised never to let go is the same God who is calling you today. Not to earn his love. You can't. Not to prove your worth. He's already settled that. But to trust him, to offer your life as a living sacrifice, and to step into the story he's been writing since before the world began.

The gospel is the power of God for salvation to everyone who believes.

That includes you.

www.ingramcontent.com/pod-product-compliance
Lightning Source LLC
Chambersburg PA
CBHW050955050726
47592CB00007B/2577